Finding
Courage to Change

By Ana Megrelishvili

Finding Courage to Change

Website: www.findcouragetochange.com

Cover Design by: Salome Merabishvili

Photography by: Brian Christian

Edited by: Jennifer Wright (The Author's Way Publishing)

ISBN: 979-8-9885829-0-8 (Paperback)

Finding Courage to Change

Table of Contents

Introduction

I wrote this book during my sabbatical year that I took in 2022. I decided that I needed to take my own "Eat, Pray, Love" journey to find my authentic self. This desire came after I realized that I lived my entire life based on my upbringing, cultural expectations, childhood trauma and the image I have built of who I should be.

I was 33 years old and did not know who I really was. I, originally, thought the purpose of this book was to put everything that has happened in my life in writing to achieve healing. However, later I realized that for me to achieve full closure, my past pain and trauma must mean something. It must have a purpose. Otherwise, it was all for nothing. I know that each experience has shaped me into a woman who I am today, but I wanted to look at the world beyond me. This book is my small contribution to better this world. If I can help even one other soul by sharing my experience and what I learned, then this book has achieved its purpose. If I can make one reader feel that they are not alone in what they are currently going through, my life has been purposeful.

My prayer for this book is that it will give its reader a glimmer of hope that their pain does not have to define them and that they can thrive as a survivor of the trauma they've been through or are still in the midst of. Your pain can become the source of your power if you use it for the good. I was able to leave the past in the past and move into the future and so can you! I believe in you with all my heart! Thank you for picking up this book and finding the courage to seek change.

Chapter 1:

What I Learned from Who I Became

Due to how dominant my father was, his behavior left me with no room to express myself or exert my will as a child. It felt like I existed for the first sixteen years of my life as a shell of who I truly was. Because of my freedom loving nature, it was especially painful and stifling for me to experience such overshadowing of my father's will over my own. I often wonder if he sensed my naturally intense and passionate nature. What about that nature caused him to discipline me in his own twisted ways and control me through unreasonable rules and restrictions?

When the rules and restrictions did not work, he resorted to shaming and guilt as a secondary way to control me. My father has an incredibly low tolerance for expression of emotions. This might have been his way to diminish and confine what he did not understand as I had a deep emotional nature from a very young age. Instead of dealing with my feelings and emotions, I had to suppress them to function and survive. This was damaging to me as an adult as I had struggled with expressing my strengths and did not show how I truly felt.

Later, it resulted in an upside-down shift where I constantly tried to show that I was in control. Often it was my irrational desire to finally prove that I could do whatever I wanted. It took me many years of self-development before I healed this trauma of not being able to express myself when I was younger and found a healthy outlet for my desire for freedom. I had to recognize in myself that I don't like rules, restrictions or anything that gets in the way of my freedom.

The betrayal and violation I experienced from my family has left me with deep wounds, lack of self-love and vulnerability. I often felt alone, thinking no one understood what I had gone through. It is a common behavior to feel like your trauma is unique to you and this emotion causes victims to feel alienated and want to keep it hidden from everyone else. It was mind-blowing to me to find out how many women in my life have gone through various traumatic events in their lives. Once I became aware of where my wounds were and I faced them, I allowed myself to share my experiences with other people. My vulnerability, in return, opened up space for them to discuss their own experiences with trauma. Before we knew it, we created a safe space for us to heal together.

Once I accepted the pain and discomfort in the process around the person I am becoming, I began to heal myself and help others. I encourage everyone in my life to have the courage to come out of the shadows and start the healing process when they feel ready. It is like an ignition making me incorporate what I have learned and share it with others.

I try to lead by example, and I am an open book for my friends. They know many of the stories I am about to share in this book, and I am always open to discuss anything from my past. I refuse to allow these traumatic experiences to remain just that - traumas. I want to use what I went through for good and if I can help even one person by sharing my story, then this book has achieved its purpose. I will never again view myself as a victim. That is no longer who I am. My struggles have become the source of my greatest strength. I have used the pain of my past as an integrated part of who I am today and that gives me a powerful perspective and wisdom. I want to use this wisdom and knowledge as a healing elixir for the souls of other people struggling today.

From a very young age, my focused ambitions and serious side took over and that was what helped me achieve everything in my life. My poor socio-economic upbringing made me feel deficient and in order to feel on par with others, I often felt that I had to compensate and prove myself worthy. I put pressure on myself to succeed and to achieve what others only have dreamed of. When I look back at my life and the circumstances where I came from and compare it to where I am now, I am still amazed that I was able to achieve this. It often feels like I have lived two completely separate lives in one lifetime. However, no matter the achievements, it was a common thread in my life that it was difficult for me to enjoy the fruits of my labor. No matter how many goals I have checked off my list, it did not change the fact that I constantly felt like something was missing from my life. This was the hardest part of the development process: discovering that even when I achieved the ultimate success that I envisioned, it was not enough to fill the void and relieve this insatiable desire for more. This illusive notion of what's next is what keeps so many of us running after something that is always just out of our reach.

2023 feels like a turn into a new stage of my life, and I am excited to see where I will end up. The biggest lesson I have learned is that nothing external will deliver the gratification, happiness, fulfillment, and self-love that I've been looking for. I have been able to give all of that to myself through my faith and through love I give and receive from people in my life.

In this book, I will be detailing my sabbatical journey to healing. I needed to experience this journey to have this breakthrough and learn to love myself unconditionally. I needed to embrace my playful and youthful side. This year

I've done things I would have never allowed myself to do in the past and I will share those experiences with you.

I embraced that part of me that never wants to grow up and let her out into the world to play for the first time in my life. I have never felt as free and happy as I have felt throughout the year of my sabbatical.

Our traditions and upbringing often make us feel judged if we don't stick with established paths and how things have always worked or if we don't put down roots and focus on being practical and responsible. Like a house of cards, I have broke down my conventional lifestyle when I quit my cushiony job and walked away from the life I established in Atlanta, Georgia. I made the time to embrace my creativity and passions and find my purpose. I made time to have fun and let my curiosity and intuition to guide me. The life I am living today is beyond what I could have dreamed of before. The scariest part is that I did not even know what I was missing, I just knew that I was dissatisfied with the life I had. I could have missed out on the biggest adventure of my life if I had not taken this leap of faith.

Where I thought I would end up is not at all where I am heading and that is okay. I have learned to live in the moment and only worry about the next eminent step instead of thinking through many steps ahead like a chess player. I learned that I am not meant to conform to what society dictates and that I can make my own path and impact on this world. I allowed myself to spend time dreaming, envisioning, and imaging what happiness and purpose mean to me. I learned that it is okay for me to want to remove myself from what makes me feel boxed in and does not allow me to be my authentic self. I have created an opportunity to heal myself and through this process help others deal with their own pain by passing on the lessons that I have learned. I treat my past experiences as a sacred gift meant to be shared with others and that is the whole purpose of this book.

I want to pass on the message to everyone who would listen that change is good. It is the process that we need in order to evolve, heal, and grow. Know that the pain that you have felt and might still feel will not be permanent. That pain won't be purposeless. Join me in being an agent of change, pushing people outside of their comfort zones, so that they could reach their full potential and find healing. Walk with me on this exciting journey called Life.

Chapter 2:

The Beginning of My Story

Let me begin with a story of how I was born because it is a unique one. Upon graduation from high school, my mother learned that she was pregnant. It was an unplanned pregnancy. She was about to leave her hometown, Gori, Georgia in Eastern Europe to go to Moscow, Russia to become a first-year college student. My father was sent to Siberia to be in the Soviet army for 2 years. My mother managed to keep her pregnancy a secret from her family for several months. In February 1988, she took a plane from Moscow to Siberia and by some miracle or curse my father agreed to marry her. She came back as a married woman and told everything to my grandmother who immediately disowned her. My mother was extremely anxious throughout her pregnancy. She was experiencing this pregnancy completely on her own. In fact, my father did not even meet me for the first time, until I was almost two years old.

The Soviet army was unapologetically strict when it came to rules and did not allow my father to leave even when I was born. All qualified young men had to serve their two years in the army upon graduation from high school before they were honorably discharged.

My mother was eight months pregnant when she reconciled with my grandmother. They decided that my mother should give birth in Gori, Georgia. They took a train from Moscow in June of 1988. I was not due for another month, so they thought they were in the clear for travel. The overall trip should have been 3 days long, but we never finished the journey on that particular train. I was too impatient to meet this world and my mother went into labor on the train. They were in the middle of nowhere and the train could not stop. The conductor made an announcement asking for any doctors and nurses to proceed to the train car where my mother was. Surprisingly, there were quite a few on that train. My mother received better medical attention than she would have at the hospital. I was successfully born.

When the train arrived at the closest city of Tula, Russia, the ambulance was already waiting for us, and we were taken to the hospital for observation. Three days later, we were discharged from the hospital, and we finally arrived in Gori. I received a nickname, Matarebela, which translates from Georgian language as "born on the train".

Most of my childhood trauma was caused by my father. He grew up in a highly abusive environment himself. My grandfather was a violent alcoholic who found new ways to humiliate his four children beyond the trauma they experienced by watching their mother being constantly beaten by him. My grandfather's favorite 'lesson' in obedience for his children was to wake them up at 3 a.m. in the morning on a school night, line them up in front of him and for them to wash his feet as he was laughing at them.

Fast forward to the fact that my father did not participate in my mother's pregnancy, and he did not really raise me as a baby. He had absolutely no investment of energy into me and sometimes I even wonder if he ever truly comprehended that he was indeed my father. I don't have many memories of my childhood before my brother was born. From photos, it looks like my life was pretty okay until I was about seven years old. My brother was born when I was 6.5 years old and that's when my life was changed.

He was a wanted continuation of my father's last name, so everything revolved around him. Something changed though. My father started drinking heavily and I was 7 when I saw my mother with bruises on her face for the first time. She was sitting at the kitchen table, and I remember my father was smiling guiltily… but smiling at her! I think maybe his sadistic tendencies were hidden for a while, but they awoke that day and it only got worse from then on. My mother never worked and was fully dependent on my father financially. My father experienced no consequences to his behavior due to my mother's dependency. I remember sometimes he would leave us for days without money or food and my mother did not know where he was and there were no cell phones back then.

I was eight years old when our hunger got so bad that my mother sent me outside to go gather empty glass bottles so that I could take them to a recycling plant and get enough money to buy a loaf of bread for us. It was one of these outings when I was at the recycling plant and these two boys made fun of me for having to do that. I remember this kind lady working there who smiled at me and told me not to worry about these boys and gave me double the money that she owed me so that I did not have to keep doing it for that day. It was that day when I promised myself that I would never be poor when I grew up. Wealth acquisition became my primary goal in life that day.

The feeling of hunger was constant. I am still ashamed as an adult that I had to steal food from my classmates during this period of my life in order to survive. Hunger clouds your judgment and morals, and I can certainly understand why certain crimes happen. When you feel so desperate, you forget about anything but satisfying your hunger.

My mother was not the best teacher of morals. I remember one time she sent me as an eight-year-old girl to steal dill from some gardens that were around since she needed it for a soup that she was making but we did not have any money to buy it. I just remember the fear I felt having to climb over fences. I did not know exactly what dill looked like. I brought fennel instead and she screamed so much at me and told me I was an idiot for not knowing what dill looks like.

Desperation clouded my mother's judgement on the type of behavior she was teaching and encouraging her daughter to do. This trauma of constant hunger, morphed into a specific behavior that I had to overcome as an adult. For many years, I had to have my entire pantry and refrigerator fully stocked with food or I felt like something bad was going to happen. I was in my early thirties when I finally got over this fear of scarcity. However, I don't think I will ever be able to go on any type of a diet. Any time there is a possibility of not having food when I might want to have food, it causes my anxiety level to raise even though logically I understand that this lack of food is intentional and self-imposed.

It is important to truly understand your triggers, so that they can be healed and managed in a healthy way.

Things continued to get worse when my father would grace us with his presence at home, he started coming into my room in the middle of the night. First, he would just stare at me but eventually he would start taking my hand and use it to masturbate himself. I just remember this smell of alcohol mixed with cigarettes and constant fear of going to sleep. One night, I think the feeling of being grossed out overpowered my fear of him and I jumped up in bed and started crying. He quickly put his penis back into his underwear and told me I was having a bad dream, but these late-night visits stopped.

There were some additional behaviors that resulted from this trauma that I had to work on. Up until recently, I always slept on my stomach with a pillow on top of my head. That was the way I learned to sleep and feel somewhat protected, and it took over 20 years for me to get out of this protective habit. I was having trouble with sex as well. Sex was always somewhat painful and uncomfortable for me. This is a common trauma response of a survivor of child sexual abuse. The penetration felt like a violation to my inner child, and I was never able to fully relax and enjoy myself as an adult. The physical pain went away once I healed my pain and forgave my father.

Now at this point in my story, many people wonder about my father and how someone who is supposed to love and protect me could do something like that. Trust me, I've been pondering this question myself for many years. And it boils down to a commonly used phrase: "Hurt people hurt people." As an abused victim, my father became an abuser as an adult. I was actually a rare statistic of people who break the cycle of violence. I had strength in me given by God and a thought that he planted in me when I was a child when I heard: "You are meant for more than this life". My purpose for the longest time was to NOT become like my father. It was quite a journey to find this healing that I feel now.

It is a devastating reality that we live in the world where one in four adults experienced some sort of abuse in their childhood. This is an official statistic, but I truly believe the reality is much worse and it is over 50% of adults have experienced sexual, physical, or emotional abuse in their lifetime. The more I share my story with people in my life, the more similar stories I hear told back to me. The saddest part is that the majority of the time, this violence came from a person who the victim knew. It is not some stranger in the dark alley. I am thankful that I did not became an abuser myself. It took many years of putting my energy toward healing of my soul and my hope is that I could become a guide to other hurt souls who come in my path so that I could help them move toward healing.

I was hit by my father many times for things I did not find justifiable for such violence. For instance, I was made fun of by kids for having a lot of hair and so, I shaved my legs when I was a teenager. Apparently, I was not allowed to do that, and I was physically abused to show his displeasure with me. I was not allowed to pierce my ears or get rid of my almost unibrow. My body did not belong to me. I had no freedom to alter anything in my appearance without my father's permission. My father made fun of me for my thick knees when I gained weight during puberty, and I was not allowed to sing in his presence. I never sang in front of other people until I was 28 when I first had the courage to sing karaoke in public as a dare. Now I recognize that this kind of upbringing is abnormal, and I was under a lot of psychological and physical abuse from my father. I just remember never feeling like I had any power or control over my life or any of my decisions. I did not belong to myself.

I was existing, not living. My escape was through books. I read a lot as I could almost forget my own reality and transform myself into one of the characters in the book I was reading. Now, as an adult, freedom of choice is not something I would ever let anyone take away from me and I would never take that away from someone else. Freedom of choice can never be taken for granted. God gave it to us and trust me when I tell you that your soul will hurt if it is ever taken away from you.

There were times when I was asked to babysit my little cousin who was less than two years old when I was a teenager. One day, I was carrying him down the stairs to go for a walk and I twisted my ankle and fell. I remember that even at that age, my protective instinct did not hesitate even for a second and I did all I could to protect my cousin from the impact to the ground in detriment to myself. I got hurt pretty badly but made sure that I protected his little head. Of course, the fall scared the baby and he started crying. His mother rushed down and took him upstairs to examine him. I followed them up scared that I might have really hurt him. As soon as I walked in, I received a strong hit to my head by my father. My ears started ringing and I started crying from pain. He was screaming at me and hitting me until my grandmother finally came out and told him to leave me alone. I laid down on a couch, crawled into a ball, hugging my knees and cried. My little cousin walked over to me and put his little hand on my head to try to comfort me.

The baby showed me compassion that my father did not show me even though I was already physically hurt from the fall. I was also emotionally terrified that I might have accidently caused harm to a small innocent child. Looking back now, I understand that he had that same fear, but he could not process his feelings any other way but with violence that was directed toward the person who caused him to have this fear - me.

My Godmother asked me once if I had any good memories associated with my father. I had to pause for a long time to try to dig for any and in the end, I could not find any. Even events that should have been happy and joyful would be ruined by my father's alcoholism or by his lack of compassion.

There are two stories from celebrations that stick out in my memory. The first story is from New Year's when I was fourteen. I should have loved New Year's because of all the delicious food and presents that I received. In Georgia, New Year's Eve is the biggest celebration of the year. There was great food and we exchanged gifts at midnight. However, I dreaded the New Year's Day every year. My family forced me to wash all the dishes as soon as I woke up on New Year's Day. That was a lot of dishes. That particular year, I woke up extremely sick. Shortly after I got up, I threw up and then had to lay down because I felt so weak. It was not even five minutes later when my father marched into my room angrily: "Get up and go clean up your throw up. Who is going to clean it up after you? And then go wash all the dishes. They are not going to wash themselves!" I could barely stand on my feet as I washed those dishes.

When I reflect back, this made me feel so unloved and unprotected. No matter what was wrong with me, I was not worthy of care and love. I was expected to perform, and I was only useful when I make other people's lives better and easier. I have carried this thought process for a long time and right into my adult relationships. I have always been one to give to everyone in my life and then felt resentful for it. Being a giver will attract a lot of takers if you do not protect yourself from being taken advantage of. I only recognized this pattern in myself two years ago and now consciously work on truly believing in every cell of my body and every neuron in my brain that I am worthy of being loved for who I am, not for what I can bring to the table.

The second celebration story was from my eighteenth birthday party. My father decided to splurge and celebrate my birthday at a restaurant. My birthdays weren't typically celebrated in a big way like that in my family. I was so excited. I had my hair done in the salon and I was wearing a beautiful red dress.

Everything was going smooth for a while until my father hit that alcohol threshold. It almost felt like some sort of a demon got inside of him. I could tell when this was happening, I just never knew who this aggression would spill over to. This time it was directed toward the men sitting at the table next to us. My father's demon decided that they "looked at me funny" and he had to protect me from these lustful men. My father was drinking Turkish coffee and then suddenly threw the cup at these men. Luckily it landed on the ground before hitting anyone and it shattered to pieces. I still remember that moment when happiness gets an abrupt pause. The energy of the room shifted. I realized that here we go again with him ruining every happy memory that I could potentially have. What followed next was a lot of screaming, people holding my father back, us paying our bill hastily and going home. The party was over. My birthday is ruined once again. Thanks dad!

As an adult, I now celebrate my birthdays in a big way. Every year, I come up with a new idea for how I am going to celebrate, and it always involves all my friends being with me. I celebrate being alive, having an opportunity to bring people I love together but I also give this opportunity to my little girl inside of me to experience the kinds of birthdays she never got to experience growing up. I give this gift to myself because I feel that it is much needed as part of my healing process. I will continue this until I feel otherwise. If one year, I wake up feeling like I don't want a big to do for my birthday, I will know that my little girl is all grown up and healed.

Chapter 3:

Growing up as an Outsider

My family and I lived in Moscow, Russia from the time I was born until I was twelve. Growing up in Russia during that time was challenging. At that time, Russia was in the midst of the war with Chechnya. Tension toward people from the Caucasus Mountain regions was palpable. I, of course, did not look like an average Russian girl with blond hair and blue eyes, so I felt that aggression even as a child. Many Russians have this favorite expression they like to use to this day toward people who looked like me - 'Chernojopaia'- that translates as the one who has a black ass. I cannot tell you how many times I have heard this expression used toward me. Children have spat on me. I even once had gypsies chase after me as I was walking home from school asking me to join them. They called me "Sister." I was terrified going to school after this incident as I was always sent to walk alone. I am still amazed that I was able to maintain all As in school and was an excellent student with everything I had going on at home and outside of it.

Nobody at home bothered to sit with me and provide me with any help. I was left alone to do my studies. Even as a young child, I would come home after school and would go straight into my bedroom to do homework, I would not do anything else until my schoolwork was completed.

I have felt like an outsider in the society in which I was growing up and I always considered myself ugly. I did not look like anyone around me at school. I never dressed particularly well as my parents could not afford to buy me many outfits. I was rotating the same three outfits that I had and never thought anything of it. As long as my clothes were clean was all that mattered. I really liked my long curly hair. I had thick black hair that went down to below my waist.

When I was seven, as it often happens with children, there was an outbreak of lice in my school. I was exposed to the lice and brought some home. Many parents would have gotten the special shampoo and painstakingly cleaned my hair of the lice. My parent took the easier route and cut all of my hair off. I had a buzz cut once they were done with me. My beautiful hair was no more. I cried as I looked at myself in the mirror. My ugliness was screaming at me louder than ever. My parents' response was that this was the consequence of my own actions of not being careful and bringing lice home. I still shiver looking at my photos from that time.

Any of my extra-curricular activities that I enjoyed were short lived as we constantly moved from place to place. As a child, I loved ballet lessons and theater. Those were moments when I felt normal and happy and free to express myself. It broke my heart every time I was taken out of those activities because we moved or because we could not afford it anymore. And I can never forget how much it broke my heart when I was forbidden to go to my theater lessons because I got a B on one of my tests.

My happy childhood moments are associated with a tall tree that grew in front of our apartment building. I learned to climb it and each time, I became braver and braver and climbed higher and higher up that tree. When I close my eyes, I can still see the green leaves on the branches and how peaceful I felt up there. The hustle and bustle of busy Moscow streets disappeared up in my tree. There, I could dream about little things that my heart desired. One day I climbed the highest I've ever climbed and the branch that I was on was too weak to support me. I felt it give underneath me and it started to bend. Luckily, I reacted quickly and crawled back toward the tree trunk and went down the level. My guardian angel was watching over me that day because if I would have fallen from that branch, I would have been dead or an invalid for the rest of my life. Thank you, God, for watching over me then and always.

One day, when I was 9, I returned from school to find the door to the kitchen closed and my mother sitting on the chair crying as she was talking to my father. This was not the regular situation where she was crying because of what my father has done or said. This was a situation where my father was sober and comforting her. I got really scared. Eventually my mother came out of the kitchen and called me to come in. I walked in slowly wondering if I had done something to upset her. She proceeded to tell me that they must take me to the hospital where I would need to stay for a few days. My immune system had become affected by mal-nutrition and the stress I was experiencing at home and at school. I had contracted tuberculosis.

I didn't comprehend what it really meant. I can say that I was extremely happy for those few days I had to spend at the hospital. I felt safe. I got to spend time with other kids. My mom would come visit me every day to do schoolwork together and she made me my favorite pie that I got to eat every day while at the hospital. I honestly did not want to leave and go back home after those few days.

That experience with Tuberculosis left me so that every time I took the TB skin test, I would come back positive. Because of that positive test, when I came to the US as an adult, I had to undergo a special course of pills for twenty days. I had to do this so that I could have a special paper that states I am not contagious. What a lovely way to begin your life in the new country!

Later that year, we moved outside of Moscow to a little town on the outskirts because we no longer could afford rent in Moscow. We lived in a one-bedroom apartment and suddenly my father's sister and her family had to come live with us. We now had four adults, two 9-year-old girls (me and my cousin were born two months apart), my 4-year-old male cousin and my 2.5-year-old brother who were all living in a one-bedroom apartment for months. My cousin and I slept on the floor in the kitchen that was full of cockroaches. I loved that kitchen anyway because my cousin and I would play a cassette tape of our favorite singer, Valeri Meladze, turn off the lights and dance to his songs. Those were moments of happiness and joy where reality ceased to exist while music was going, and we were dancing.

After about a year, we got an upgrade and moved into a two-bedroom apartment where each family had their own bedroom. We lived like this for almost a year. The bright light during this time were moments when my cousins and I would build forts out of couch cushions and blankets and crawl in to daydream together.

There was constant tension between my aunt and my mother, though. They eventually got into such a big fight that my aunt said horrible things that she wished would happen to me and my brother. Georgians are very superstitious and when a person puts a curse on children, that is not taken lightly. That was the straw that broke the camel's back, and my aunt's family moved out soon after this fight. It was my parents, my brother and I yet again.

I have very few memories from this period of time but the few that I do have made a big impact on me. One particular memory is regarding my aunt. As we were poor, candies and sweets were a rarity for us to receive as children. That one particular evening, my uncle and my father came back and brought whole bunch of candies for us, the kids. I was so excited and could not hide my excitement. It was short-lived because I remember my aunt looking at me with this expression of disgust on her face. Even as a child, I could read her disapproval of my extreme excitement. And just like that, she killed that happy excited girl inside of me. I just remember shriveling under her eyes and becoming sad because I felt judged.

Another memory was in regard to the constant unspoken competition that my cousin and I were forced into by our parents. As we were in the same classroom, our grades were compared daily and whoever did worse that day was shamed. Our personalities were polar opposite. Despite everything that was going on around me, I was full of life and excitement. I loved dancing and performing. My cousin was quiet and reserved and always reading. They called her wise and called me a troublemaker. By the time we reached puberty, I was told by my grandparents that I would not account for anything but to get married by age fifteen, have babies and serve my husband. My cousin, on the other hand, was called a child sage and was told that she would reach heights unknown to anyone in our family. Oh, how wrong their predictions ended up being.

Two more years passed, and my father was able to add even more "excitement" into our lives. He managed to owe a lot of money to some member of the Russian mafia. During that time, he would leave us for days. When he was gone, we would have to tiptoe to our apartment because every so often scary looking guys would show up and start banging on our door looking for my father. We lived in constant fear and watched over our backs in case someone was following us home. At ten, I was told to watch if anyone was following me into the house and as I was walking up the stairs to our apartment on fifth floor. When I reached the fourth floor, I was told to stop and listen to make sure no one was waiting by our apartment door. I had to creep up slowly to make sure the coast was clear, and I could knock the special knock to let my mother know that it was me coming from school. At some point, the harassment got so bad, that my mother took my brother and I to stay with one of her friends in Moscow. Those two days felt like paradise for me. I was well fed, could play video games, and did not have to be scared that some scary man is right outside the door waiting for us.

The following year as I turned eleven, my father added a new way of tormenting my mother where he would pretend that he wanted to kill himself and my mother needed to stop him. I say pretend because he would conveniently grab the dullest knife to cut his veins. This one time, I was awakened by screams coming from the balcony. I ran out to see what was going on and saw that this time my father was "committing suicide" by jumping from the balcony. My mother was still in her night gown, hanging onto my father's belt and trying to pull him back in. She was screaming for me to help her. I just remember freezing as I watched what was happening and thinking, "Just let him do it," but my mother was playing the role of a savior in this scenario or a role of a victim when my father was the abuser.

I think the only reason I decided to help my mother is because the weight of my father started to pull her after him and so I ran up and helped her pull him back down. I was ready to lose him but not her. The craziest part is that once my parents both played their roles and got the next hit of adrenaline, they went on with their day like nothing happened. None of the incidents were ever discussed. My mother never slowed down to ask me how I was doing after these traumatic incidents. Everything was just swept under the rug. Nobody in my mother's life knew of anything that was happening in our family. She was a firm believer that family's dirt needs to be kept inside. On the outside, she maintained an image of a perfectly normal and happy family.

My father is a twin and his brother decided to visit us one year. My uncle was a drug addict who came out of jail not long before. Reflecting on this, I don't know why my father thought it was a good idea to allow his brother into our house and our lives. After a month of living with us, my father took my uncle to his job. He was one of the partners of the store and my father wanted to show off his newly found success with his brother.

My uncle took notice of it. A few days later my uncle was gone unexpectedly, and my father was taken to jail. Turns out, my uncle pretended to be my father, walked into the store where my father was a partner and stole all the money from cash registers. He then disappeared and my father was the one who was taken to jail. It took months of explaining and trying to prove that my father's twin was the one who committed the crime. I loved this period of time, even though my mother was so distraught by this whole situation. I did not have to worry about my father coming into my room at night or about any of his drunken shenanigans. My mother finally had to tell my grandmother what was happening, and my grandmother came to stay with us. When she realized that it would take months before my father would be released, she took time off from her job in Georgia and got a job as a baker in Russia, so that she could stay with us and take care of us.

My grandmother always showed her love with actions and this situation was no exception. Eventually, the agreement was reached that my father would have to return all the stolen money and forgo his share of the business and then they would drop all the charges. My family did not have that kind of money. My father's family did not step up to help either. They told him that he should have known better than to allow a drug addict into his life. Therefore, it was again my grandma who sold all the gold jewelry she had acquired throughout her life, so that my father could be released from jail. The agreement was that if she were to do that, then we would have to leave Russia and relocate to Georgia to be close to my grandma.

Chapter 4:

Starting Over in Georgia

Living in Russia, I always felt like an outsider, and Russians would never let me forget that I was Georgian - not one of them. When I was twelve and my family finally decided to move back to Georgia, I felt like an outsider once again. My parents never taught me to speak the Georgian language. Georgian language has its own alphabet. It is a language not related to any other language in the world. So here I was in my home country feeling like an alien again. Luckily my grandmother immediately hired me a tutor in the Georgian language and within a year I was almost fluent.

My grandmother, Natela, from my mother's side, has a special place in my heart. She had many issues as a mother raising my mother but to me, she was the best grandma. The couple of summers I was able to spend with her in Georgia were the highlights of my childhood. Some of my happiest moments are associated with her. She was my safe haven and the place where I felt loved. She loved food, going to see people as a guest and dressing up. She did not care about what society would think of her in her decision making. Her weakness was her love of fortune tellers as she spent a lot of her money on that. I am often told that I have many qualities of my grandmother. She was the one who taught me how to cook and be a hostess. She was the one who taught me how to enjoy life.

My grandmother did not have an easy childhood and that shaped her into the woman and mother that she became to my mother. This cycle of trauma on my mother's side of the family actually started with my great grandmother. I was named after her, but I spell my name with one n- Ana. She was a blue-eyed beautiful Russian teenager when she met the father of my grandmother who was stationed at the military base close by. He was from Gori, Georgia and when his serving time was up, he brought my great grandmother from Russia with him with a promise of marrying her in Georgia. My grandmother was conceived but the promise of marriage never materialized as his parents did not want a Russian daughter-in-law. My great grandmother, Anna, was left alone with a daughter on the way and no financial support. Anna became a waitress in the only hotel in town to be able to raise my grandmother as a single mother. She struggled financially, and my grandmother was often hungry. She was often seen running behind trucks carrying cabbage, picking up some cabbage leaves that would drop and eating them. She experienced this while knowing that her father is living in the same town and was married and raising another child who is fully provided for while she is starving.

Anna was known to be a calm, quiet woman who would not harm an ant. There is a Russian saying that goes something like this: In a quiet pond reside demons. This saying applied to Anna in the story I am about to share. When my grandmother was a teenager, my great grandmother, Anna, fell in love with a customer who used to frequent the restaurant where she worked. Her love was so strong and blinding that when she found out that this man was seeing another woman, she acted out in an unthinkable way. She learned that woman's schedule, waited for her one evening and threw acid into her face, disfiguring her forever. That woman had two adult sons who raped my grandmother as a revenge. A horrific end of the story. I only learned about this recently from my grandmother's best friend. What a violent way for your virginity to be taken away from you. My grandmother never received any type of therapy as this story had to be swept under the rug. My grandmother immediately dropped out of school, and nobody knew the reason behind this. This is a story that most people who knew Anna would not believe because of the impression she left with everyone. However, in a quiet pond reside demons indeed.

By the time I knew my great grandmother, she was already very frail. Years of standing on her feet and running around as a waitress took a toll on her body. She was laying down most of the time and only got up to eat or to go to the bathroom. My grandmother took care of all of Anna's physical needs, but I never remember them having any communication beyond my grandmother barking some order to her mother on what she wanted her to do.

Despite this kind of interaction, my grandmother fought relentlessly when my great grandmother had a heart attack. Anna became unconscious and my grandmother brought the best doctors from the capital and paid exorbitant amounts of money to give the best medical care to her mother. As Anna was in this state where doctors could not wake her up, my grandmother would not leave her side. In the middle of the night, Anna began to speak out loud in her dream state. From what my grandma could make out, Anna was in this long queue of people. She would constantly let other people go in front of her in line and say that it was not her turn yet to go. "No, no, you go ahead. It is not my turn yet" was the line she kept repeating. This story was told in my family as proof that there is life after death, and you don't go into nothingness. I'd like to believe that my great grandmother was lining up into queue to heaven, but God told her time on earth was not completed yet.

Let me continue uncovering the cycle of trauma within my family. As my grandmother became a student at a university, she met my mother's father. They fell in love and as a result my mother was conceived. Unfortunately, the story had to repeat itself and he never fulfilled his promise of marrying my grandmother as his parents wanted someone different for him as his wife. My grandmother was devasted and considered getting an abortion. However, she never made any important decisions without consulting a fortune teller first. This particular fortune teller told her that she would never have children if she went through with this abortion and thus, my grandmother decided to keep the child- my mother. She would often remind my mother about this decision as part of her control technique. It made my mother feel unwanted. Like the only reason why my grandmother decided to keep her was because of the fortune teller.

These experiences with men caused my grandmother to create a hard exterior and close herself off. She refused to show any sign of weakness or femininity. She was known in town as a tough woman who nobody messed with. She was raising my mother, so that she would have anything that she needed and wanted except her mother's affection. No physical or verbal affection was given to my mother as she was growing up. The only time my grandmother would allow any affection is when she thought my mother was asleep. At night, when she thought my mother was asleep, my grandma would walk over to my mother and kiss her on the head. She did not know that my mother only pretended to be asleep when she did this so that she could experience that one moment of affection. My mother lived for those moments. The rest of the time, she was raised in fear of my grandmother.

The father figure that my mother had in her life came when she was nine years old. His name was Jim. My grandmother fell in love with Jim - a married man who loved her back. As it often goes, he had no intention of leaving his wife and his family. Divorce was an absolute taboo in Georgia at that time. Affairs were also taboo, but divorce trumped affairs and thus, their relationship lasted until Jim's death. Their relationship lasted over twenty-five years.

The memory I had of this man was from the time I would spend summers with my grandmother. She was not a morning person and loved to sleep in, but she would wake up early to get ready when she knew that her Jim was coming to see her. He would always come before work and bring fresh bread for her. She would always greet him with a fresh cup of Turkish coffee and kisses all over his face. She looked like a giddy teenage girl who blossomed when he was in her presence. Even as a child, I knew that something special was happening as I have never seen my grandmother as happy as when she was with him. I knew that they truly loved each other. It is tough to reconcile now as an adult the fact that what was happening between them was an act of adultery and it was wrong. Yet, the love that they felt for each other was obvious to a young child. I still struggle with knowing that what they did was absolutely wrong but yet knowing that he was the only man who brought happiness to my grandmother throughout her life.

When Jim passed away, my grandmother was not able to say her goodbyes as she was not permitted to attend the funeral and that broke her. Her mental and physical health began to quickly deteriorate. She had Alzheimer's disease and diabetes in the last four years of her life. Her childhood trauma of experiencing hunger manifested as a compulsive eating habit. She quickly gained a lot of weight and diabetes caused her to develop a gangrene in her leg. Eventually her leg had to be amputated. She experienced so much pain that it caused her to no longer be herself. She cried and moaned non-stop and called her daughter: "Mother."

My mother was her caretaker throughout those four years. She took care of her not because of love or care but because of the obligation that she felt. They screamed at each other and said many painful words that they never could take back. The last words that my grandmother said to my mother before she passed away were: "Go away, stupid!" My mother carries anger and resentment toward my grandmother to this day. My hope is that when she reads this book one day, it will help her see the pattern of dysfunctional relationships that have been passed on generation to generation and she will try to let go of these negative feelings she has been carrying all her life.

My grandmother experienced betrayal many times in her life but she always loved people in her own unique way and never lost faith in humanity. My grandmother's trust had been broken once again when she found out that one of her closest friends had been lying to her by selling cheap jewelry to her at double the price. She would tell my grandmother lies about how valuable and well-made the jewelry was. Her trauma and betrayals caused her to shut down the gentle part of her that only came out when she became a grandmother. I experienced what she could have been if not for what she had to go through. In turn, my mother wanted to escape my grandmother's authoritarian regime and jumped straight into a lion's den when she married my father.

When we moved back to Gori, Georgia, my grandmother gave us a one-bedroom apartment to live in. During this period of time, I would spend half of the week with my grandma and half of a week with my father's parents and maybe just a day at home. Anything I could do to be out of the house, I was ready to do it. I was going to the only Russian school in town and was placed in a class full of rich kids or children of teachers- the elite of our school. I and two other girls moved from different parts of Russia to Gori that same year, so we became fast friends as new kids on the block. This time around, bullying in school was not because of how I looked but because of my class. I was considered to be poor and that was something they could make fun of. However, on the plus side my thoughts about my appearance started shifting in Georgia. I've always thought of myself as an ugly duckling because of my appearance and how I was made fun of in Russia. In Georgia, however, I was considered to be beautiful. All these boys suddenly started coming up to me and telling me that they liked me. I want to meet the first boy who had taught all these other boys how to express their feelings because they all did it the same way. They would pull me aside and all say the same phrase: "I love you and I am curious about your answer on how you feel." No more, no less but each of them used this exact phrase. Sometimes I never even met the boy professing his love to me when they were telling me this phrase. I was very confused for a while.

Then there was this boy who had probably stolen every flower in the neighborhood because I would wake up every day with a fresh bouquet of flowers outside the door of my house. Sometimes those bouquets still had dirt from where he pulled the flowers out of the ground. One day, he put flowers all over the balcony. I was staying with my grandparents who lived on the second floor, and he climbed up in the middle of the night to cover the entire balcony in flowers. When I rejected him, this same boy wrote that I was a witch in graffiti all over the neighborhood. That was my first lesson in love that there is a very short step from love to hate.

Another lesson came a few months later. My grandmother signed me up for some dance classes. The theater was just a block away from where she lived. The teacher was a twenty-eight-year-old man named David. He was a very tall man with bright blue eyes. I was late coming in and the rest of the kids had learned quite a bit of the choreography. The instructor decided that I needed extra lessons to make up for the time I had missed. It was the third lesson when my teacher suddenly kissed me. I was shocked on one hand and curious on the other hand. I was just thirteen years old. David explained to me that he loved me and wanted to be with me and that I should not fear anything that he did. I had just started my period that year and my body had just started to develop.

He told me that he would wait a little bit for me to grow up and then we could be together. On one hand, I was flattered, but something did not feel right. With each class, there was less and less dancing and more and more of David trying to be intimate with me while kissing and touching my young body. The feeling of disgust was developing in me stronger and stronger as he was shoving his tongue into my

46

mouth but I was too scared to stop him. Eventually I told my mother about what was happening. My mother was too afraid to tell my father as she was scared, he would do something that would cause him to end up in jail. She just allowed me to never go back to that dance class again. There were no consequences for a twenty-eight-year-old man who was abusing a thirteen-year-old girl. Even then, I knew that my mother was supposed to do something about it. Her behavior caused me to believe that I did something to provoke that behavior from David and it was my fault and responsibility. This is a common response of victims of child sexual abuse.

The story did not end with me quitting my dance classes. David had the audacity to find out where we lived. God was protecting me that day because it was extremely unusual for me to be home alone as my father did not work at that time and was always at home. I don't remember where my father was that particular day when I heard a knock at the door. I slowly creeped up to the door and looked through the peep hole to see David standing on the other side of the door. My heart was racing from fear, but I also felt relieved that my father was not at home. I was afraid of what might have happened if that conversation had taken place. David left and luckily never came back. I tried to forget this ever happened to me.

A couple years later, I learned that David ended up marrying one of his students. That girl was only fifteen years old. This girl could have been me. And my mother could have prevented this pedophile from taking advantage of another young woman if she would have raised an alarm when I told her about what happened to me. Overall, men taking young girls as brides was a normal practice back then in Georgia, and nobody blinked twice at it.

After we moved to Georgia, I felt like we were protected by my grandmother. My mother started working as a pharmacist, so I began to beg my mother to divorce my father. The power dynamic should have changed since my mother was now working and my father laid happily on the couch all day. My father was an intelligent manipulator though. He told my mother that since he supported us for so many years and she stayed at home, now it was her turn to work, and he would stay home. It was a smart tactic that my mother fell for. Now, as an adult, I often wonder if my mother ever questioned why a little girl would beg her mother to leave her own father? I wonder if she secretly knew about what I had experienced but chose to ignore it? She might not even acknowledge it to herself even now. No amount of physical and psychological abuse could shake my mother's worry about what people would say or that my brother would grow up without a father. These responses from her made me feel like my happiness was less important than everyone else's. She did not want to repeat the history of my great grandmother and grandmother and become a single mother at any cost.

These same comments and the double standards in raising me versus my brother always left me quietly angry and resentful. I could never understand why just because I am a girl, I had to do all the household chores while my brother did not have to do anything. Or why was my brother's priority of having a father higher than my safety and happiness.

When it was time for me to have my tonsils out, my father didn't want to pay the full price at the hospital. Instead, he found a doctor but a more accurate term for him should be a butcher in a white coat, who agreed to do this surgery at his house. So, at thirteen, I was seated in this green chair with my hands tied to it and there was the doctor and his assistant with me in the room who didn't give me any type of anesthesia but cut tonsil from one side of my mouth, just like that. I screamed from pain, but my screams were muffled because I was drowning in my own blood that rushed down my throat. The assistant was screaming at me angrily that I needed to calm down because they needed to do the same procedure on the other side. She held my head steady in a grip lock while my second tonsil was cut out the same way. I have no idea how I didn't pass out from pain but at the end of it all, they just told me that I might throw up because I swallowed so much blood. My father happily paid the fee and I successfully lost tonsils but added one more trauma to my arsenal. As a cherry on top, he also didn't want to pay for a taxi and made me walk home after the surgery.

As I was telling this story to my Godmother who is a doctor, her eyes kept getting wider and wider the further I got into my story. She told me that God was watching over me that day because based on the condition in which this surgery was conducted, I should have had some major complications. She said that I was already considered to be an adult by the time they decided to have this surgery and surgery is needed in very few cases at that age.

I got curious and researched the studies conducted regarding risks associated with adult tonsil removals and here is what I found:

To conduct its study, the team, which also included researchers from the Kaiser San Francisco Medical Center and Truven Health Analytics, examined data from 36,210 adult tonsillectomy patients. The results appeared in the April 2014 issue of Otolaryngology -- Head and Neck Surgery. The findings suggest that of adult patients who have undergone a tonsillectomy, 20 percent had a complication, 10 percent visited an emergency room, and approximately 1.5 percent were admitted to a hospital within 14 days of the procedure. Six percent of adult patients were treated for postoperative hemorrhage; 2 percent were treated for dehydration; and 11 percent were treated for ear, nose, or throat pain within 14 days of surgery.

And these are the current numbers with the US medical system, not the procedure I had in 2002 at a house in a third world country. It is a scary thought to realize that your parents put you in this type of danger because of their ignorance about the risks and the desire to save money.

My brother lived to annoy me as he was growing up. I was never able to reciprocate as I was the big sister and was expected to be more understanding. One day when I was babysitting him, he said something nasty and ran away from the kitchen into the other room and closed the door behind him. The door had a thick glass that I pushed on to try to open the door. I must have been really angry because next thing I know, the glass shattered, and I was blinded by blood rushing down my face. It's interesting how our protective mechanism tells us exactly the right thing to do. I am still amazed that at thirteen, I knew to put a towel against my face to try to stop the bleeding and to give instructions to my brother to dial my mother on the phone. She rushed from work and took me to our relative who was a surgeon. Again, no anesthesia and I had stitches on my nose, forehead, and cheek at the end of that visit. Now that I think about it, healthcare in Georgia was pretty traumatic at that point in time.

Did you have one particular chore or a tradition that you absolutely hated when growing up? For me it was the annual washing of the carpets that I had to do when growing up. Georgian houses typically have tile or wooden flooring, and families use carpets to put on the floor where most foot traffic is. Those carpets get dirty, and summer was the time when I had to wash them. Talk about embarrassing moments from my teenage years. My father would bring down the carpets and lay them out on the ground in the middle of the courtyard close to the water fountain that each apartment complex had. I had to use soap and special wooden stick shaped like a T to soap up the carpets first and then constantly run water on them to get all the dirt and soap out. It took hours of work while neighborhood boys would stare at me. As a teenage girl, that was the chore I dreaded the most and begged my mother to not make me do it. However, it was done every year because some traditions just do not get broken.

As I hit puberty, my father's control was to the point where I was not allowed to leave the house past 7 pm. I hardly was able to spend any time at my grandparents' house or with friends. This overprotectiveness was partially because of the attention I was receiving from boys and men.

When I was growing up "wife kidnapping" was prevalent throughout Georgia. Georgia has been a somewhat conservative society where church and religion played an important part in traditions. Having sex before marriage was unacceptable and girls had to remain virgins until marriage. However, raging hormones of boys and men drove them to literally kidnap a girl or a woman they liked. The process was as follows. A man would like a girl and would learn the pattern of her day - what time she went to school, then home or maybe to tutors. Then he would find two or three friends and a car and set a date for wife kidnapping to take place. On a set date, a girl would be following her regular routine and suddenly this car would stop right by her. Three men would jump out of the car and shove her into the back seat and the car would drive away in the direction of some mountainous village.

Many times, that girl never even knew the man who was kidnapping her. The goal was to make sure the girl was not found by her parents until the next day. The reason being, if she was away from the house overnight, that meant she was not pure anymore and it was shameful for her to come back home. She was forced to marry the man who kidnapped and raped her. If the girl was lucky and her parents found her that same day, the man who kidnapped her experienced no real consequences. In some instances, he might be beaten, but that was the worst-case scenario. The girl would be left to continue her life with this traumatic experience.

I was in 6th grade when one of my classmates was wife kidnapped. She was thirteen and the man was twenty-one. She gave birth to her son by the time she was fourteen. Her husband physically abused her, and she was divorced by the time she was eighteen with a four-year-old she had to support on her own. Georgia had no alimony system set up at that time and most men just abandoned their children in cases of divorce. My classmate became a prostitute to be able to support her child as she only had a 6th grade education. Her husband did not allow her to go back to finish school after he "wife kidnapped" her. Her family turned away from her because of her divorce and she was left on her own with a small child to support. This is just one story of so many girls who I knew growing up and whose lives got ruined by the hormones of men. My father's goal was to make sure I did not become another girl who got "wife kidnapped" and for that I am thankful to him despite the feeling of isolation that I constantly experienced.

Chapter 5:

Experiencing Life in the US

When I was fifteen, I heard of this competition in English, and I went to it without telling my parents. It was a competition for a type of exchange student program. The grand prize was a fully paid trip to the U.S. and a year living with a host family. This was the first time I had heard of the concept of an exchange year abroad. This program was called Future Leaders Exchange or FLEX and is sponsored by the State Department and still successfully operates in many countries.

It changed the trajectory of my life.

I went through 3 rounds of competition without ever telling my parents that I was doing it. I feared that my father would forbid me to go through with it and I knew in my heart that I had to win so I could leave. Before the last round, I had no other choice but to tell everything to my parents because at that point I needed a lot of information, signatures, etc. that I couldn't get without them involved. I am thankful that for the first time in her life, my mother stood up to my father and told him that they were letting me go to the United States. My grandmother helped me to get an expedited international passport and I left Georgia to go to the US when I just turned sixteen.

I was the last person in the program to be matched with a host family. Now I know that God had a special plan, but back then I was so nervous that I would not be able to go or that I knew nothing about my host family once I finally got matched. Silly me. My host family lived right outside of Denver, Colorado and they have forever changed my life. They were married for 35+ years at that point with grown children and I was their exchange student number thirteen. Thirteen has been my favorite number since. They were the first example of a happily married couple and family I had ever seen. My host mother had a voice and equal rights and decision making and I realized then that the US is where I wanted to live. During that year, they showed me more of the US than other Americans see in their entire lifetime. That year was the best year of my life, but it was not without bumps.

First bump was on Halloween night. I was supposed to learn how to curve a pumpkin. Brand new knives were taken out of packaging, and I was told to follow the outline drawn on the pumpkin to curve out the pieces. The first attempt left me with a knife that slid right onto my left thumb, and I suddenly saw a big cut and blood flowing from my finger. My host mother, Kathy, wrapped my thumb in a clean towel and we immediately rushed to the emergency room. There, I learned that I had a cut that went all the way to my bone, and I would require several stitches. I was also taught several exercises that I had to do daily in order to gain movement back in my thumb. After those stitches, I could hardly bend my thumb. Needless to say, this was my first and last attempt ever to carve pumpkins.

Second bump came in the spring when I was playing basketball during my PE class and my 6ft tall classmate elbowed my nose by accident and broke it. I was taken to the emergency room once again with a bloody nose where it was determined that my nose was broken, and I needed to see a specialist. The specialist told me an interesting piece of information I did not know about myself. Apparently, my nose has been broken before and it did not heal properly. If they were to completely correct it, then they must break it even further to reconstruct it. If they did that, it would leave me vulnerable to any type of a hit to the nose and make it easier to be broken again. I decided to forgo that option and just have the surgery that would fix the recent break so that I could breathe again. After the procedure I was back to normal few days later.

The most transformative experience during my exchange year came from outside of the US oddly enough.

My host parents were involved with Rotary International Organization and as part of their giving efforts they organized a trip to Mexico. This was a trip to a remote village in Chihuahua state, up in the mountains. We were going with a team of optometrists who were going to give eyeglasses to Tarahumara indigenous tribes living there. These indigenous people of Mexico live in extreme levels of poverty as they reside in remote areas of the country and many of them don't even speak Spanish. They speak their own native language. We had two translators with us. One that would translate from Tarahumara language to Spanish and another who would translate from Spanish to English for us.

We stayed that week with locals who hosted us. We ate what they ate and slept under the same roof. My job was to operate the device that would measure their eyesight and then take the printout to the doctor. We had brought hundreds of frames and lenses with us from the US. I came from a poor background, but nothing could have prepared me for the level of poverty I was about to witness. One specific older man stands out in my memory. He was wearing clothes that were so warn out that they looked more like rags than clothes and he had walked 3 miles barefoot because he had no shoes. He had to carry his 1-year-old grandson with him because his parents were working, and his grandfather was his babysitter. Once this man's eyeglasses were ready and he put them on, he immediately started crying. These were tears of happiness. It was the first time when he was able to actually see the face of his grandson. Before that moment, he only saw a blurry outline of his face. I had to fight back my own tears seeing such pure moment of joy.

Everything that I had to go through in my life seemed so small in comparison. I was healthy and I could see, and the feeling of gratefulness overwhelmed me. That was the first time in my life, I saw someone whose circumstances were worse than mine and it made me realize that everything in this life is relative. It is my attitude and how I view circumstances that form my identity.

Our last night before we would leave Mexico was a celebration night. The village elders made us a cake and adults were having some alcoholic drinks. Someone brought a guitar and began singing ballads and the whole room felt warm and happy. Suddenly, we see one of our translators running after the owner's little Chihuahua dog with a tortilla. Someone yelled: "Roberto, what are you doing?" Tipsy Roberto stops and with a proud smile says: "I am going to catch this Chihuahua, wrap it into my tortilla, put into microwave for 3 minutes and then…. I am going to have a HOT DOG!" Everyone rolled over laughing when they heard it, and Roberto was cut off from any more alcohol for that night. That night was the first time I experienced Latin dancing. It was love at first sight and it is my most beloved hobby now as an adult.

My first act of rebellion against my father also happened during my exchange year. I really wanted to get a tattoo and I told my host mom about it. Kathy also was planning on getting another tattoo and she said: "Why don't we get it together?" I was sixteen and Kathy had to sign a parental agreement for me to get my first and only tattoo on my left ankle. I decided to get a butterfly as a sign of transformation. I associated myself with a cocoon as my life before the US and I was transformed into a beautiful butterfly during this transformative exchange year. I very well knew that this act would cause eruption of anger from my father, but I did not care. This was my coming of age defining moment in life.

As expected, upon my return, my father was furious and made me wear pants or socks for the first couple of weeks but then everything went back to usual. Also, I was the first woman in my hometown to have a tattoo, so I was the talk of the town. Everyone was pointing fingers at my tattoo while whispering their disapproval and I loved it! Something within me got released once I got my tattoo and there was no power on this earth that could put me back into that box where I lived for the first sixteen years of my life. I do not plan to be getting any other tattoos in the future and I also haven't once regretted getting my butterfly. She has been part of me for the past eighteen years.

Finding Courage to Change

It took me several months to truly believe that I was living in the US. It often felt like I was walking in a dazed state of mind. Everything seemed so new and different. Food was different. There were so many things I'd never tasted before. Reading a menu at the restaurant was an adventure of its own. I found the US highway system fascinating as I'd never seen so many bridges and roads overlapping. I'd never seen skyscrapers before! I found it weird that Americans walked barefoot at home and sometimes even would walk barefoot on their driveways. I've never had my own bedroom until that year as I always had to share with my brother. My privacy was respected, and I felt loved and taken care of by two strangers who opened their house and their hearts to me. When it was time to go back to Georgia, I cried the entire ride to the airport, at the airport and on the plane. I did not want to leave and go back but I had to. Based on the visa requirement, I was not allowed to come back to the US for at least two years.

I did come back to the US eventually and I will describe how later but here I want to dedicate time to talk about the significance of becoming a US citizen. I came to the US the second time in August of 2008 and finally became a citizen in February of 2018. It took 10 years, thousands of dollars, and pages of paperwork, but I will never forget the day I was sworn in while raising my right hand. This is something that so many people across the world dream of and I was living it. I am a proud American and I am so proud to hold an American passport any time I fly abroad. Is the US perfect? Absolutely not, but there is no other country I'd rather live in. It is incredibly frustrating for me to hear people who are born in the US and who do not realize the advantage that they have just by being born in this country.

There are so many opportunities here that are simply not available anywhere else. If you are a hard worker and a hustler, you can make something of yourself here. There would have been no way for me to achieve even one tenth of the career success, wealth, and freedom that I was able to enjoy in this country. There are so many scholarships, governmental programs, non-profit assistance that do not exist in most countries. So many people risk their lives to cross the border into the US illegally, they leave their lives and loved ones behind for the promise of a better life that this country offers. This is not me taking a stance on illegal immigration. This is me trying to have a wakeup call for those Americans who use their life circumstances as an excuse to give up on life. If you were born in the US, be grateful for this opportunity and don't waste it. You are already a leg above most people in this world by just being an American. Carry it proudly and make the difference in your life and lives around you.

Chapter 6:

First Love

I was back in Georgia after my exchange year, and I had to take university entrance exams. I knew I had to be awarded a 100% scholarship, or I was not going to school as my parents could not pay for it. I was blessed to get it and to go to university in Tbilisi, the capital of Georgia. I was to study International Tourism. During my freshman year, I fell in love with my classmate. He was my first boyfriend and I had to hide his existence from my family. We would have to go for walks in parks to not risk being seen by someone who might know me. After taking a six-year break, my father finally started working as a night shift cook at the 24-hour restaurant, so I was alone at night.

After about a year of dating my boyfriend, I snuck him in one night and I lost my virginity at age nineteen. It was a huge taboo to lose your virginity before marriage, but I was young and in love. We were talking about marriage after graduation. This bliss did not last for a long time as somehow my father found out about my boyfriend, and I was given an ultimatum. I could either immediately break up with him or I would be kicked out of the house. I called my boyfriend in tears to tell him what happened, and he told me to pack my bags and leave. He was living with his grandmother at that point, and she told us that she would accept us. But then I saw fear in his face. I saw the realization of what this would mean and that he would be taking responsibility over me as his wife. My pride did not let me be anyone's burden so to show him grace, I told him that I would stay with my friend that night. Culturally, if I would have stayed at his house overnight, it would have meant that we were married. So that night was a defining moment in both of our lives. Truthfully, I was hoping he would come and get me from my friend's house and when I called him to tell him that my father showed up at my friend's house to take me to Gori, he did not object to that next step. That was the moment my heart broke as I felt unwanted, and I also felt so betrayed by him.

I was taken back to Gori where my father beat me so intensely that I could barely move the next day. He also took my phone away and threw a kettle of hot water at me and burned me. I was missing chunks of hair, but the worst part was my shattered heart. That was the lowest point in my life where I thought that I'd rather die than continue living this way. I was shamed and nobody in my family would talk or even look at me for days. The only person I was finally allowed to call was my host mother, Kathy, in the US.

When I told her what happened, she told me that they were planning to move to Africa for a year but maybe they needed to move to Georgia instead. My host parents saved my life a second time when a few months later they indeed moved to Georgia, and I was able to move in to live with them. The few months before then were horrible as I was forced to commute 2 hours each way from Gori to Tbilisi to go to university. My ex-boyfriend wanted to continue dating like nothing happened when he saw me again. I was shocked that he did not understand why I did not want to do anything with him. A couple of months later, I got my first job and started bringing in my own income and only went to university to pass my exams. It saved me from seeing my ex-boyfriend every day, so that my heart would begin to heal.

My host parents were volunteering their time and teaching English in Tbilisi and I loved living with them. One day, I was conducting a training at an American Library and during a lunch break, I came across this thick book that had a list of all colleges and universities in the US. I went through the entire book to find a list of colleges that offered full scholarships to international students and came back with a list of 3. That evening I researched all of them and only one college had guaranteed all the expenses paid if you were to get accepted. I knew I had to apply to Berea College. My host mother helped me fine tune my essays and I sent my application in. A few months later, I received an acceptance letter. I was finishing my third year of college only to become a freshman again, but I did not care. I was second in command of the largest non-profit in Georgia at that point with a great salary and exposure to all kinds of important contacts. In my heart, I knew I had to start my life over in the US and that I would do anything to stay there.

My host parents stayed in Georgia for another year. I am extremely proud of my host mom, Kathy, for starting a non-profit called Helping Hands. This non-profit operates successfully in Georgia to this day with a goal of educating youth about importance of volunteerism, eradicating domestic violence, and education about healthy relationships. This non-profit was on the front line to push the law that made domestic violence a crime in Georgia. Can you imagine a European society in the 21st century that still did not perceive domestic violence as anything worthy of reporting to the police? That was Georgia until 2009.

I was supposed to leave Georgia in August of 2008 to come to the US and a few days before I was going to leave the country, Russia invaded Georgia. My hometown, Gori, was completely destroyed by bombs. Russia was also using bombs that have been banned by United Nations and NATO. From my understanding, most bombs when they hit the ground either explode immediately or they don't explode at all if they fell on the ground in one piece. Russia was using the kinds of bombs that did not follow this rule. So, my hometown had whole bunch of huge holes throughout the city with unexploded bombs in them that could explode at any moment. After Russia withdrew, special Georgian forces had to be sent in to disarm these bombs.

My family and I luckily were able to escape and stay at my host parents' apartment in Tbilisi as they were in the US at that time. It's an unsettling feeling lying in bed wide awake and hearing a plane above you and wondering if that plane was about to drop a bomb on your house. Then there is this feeling of guilt that you are leaving your family behind but also a sweet relief that you are leaving all of this behind. We, humans, don't often realize how complex our feelings are and how we can feel polar opposite feelings at the same time. It is bizarre to me to be watching the news as I write this book and see history repeating itself as Russia has been in the midst of invading Ukraine for the past year. There were no consequences for anything that Russia did in Georgia and that bully just got more aggressive. As I was getting ready to leave for the US, all flights out of Georgia were canceled by all airlines due to war but one. Georgian Airways were mandated by Georgian Government to keep flights as normal and I was luckily on one of those flights out of the country and into my new life in Berea, Kentucky.

Finding Courage to Change

Berea College is a small liberal arts college in Berea, Kentucky. The unique aspect of this college is that all students who go there have 100% tuition scholarship. 10% of student body were international students like me and we had the cost of our room and board covered as well. It is one of the biggest privileges I have received in my life to have received amazing education with 0 student loans. I am grateful for the opportunity I received to study abroad as a student because that trip to this day is the travel experience that has pushed my boundaries the furthest.

I got an extremely rare opportunity to visit and stay with the Iban tribe of headhunters in Malaysia. This tribe typically does not allow any visitors to enter their villages. They speak their own language different from Malay and tribe members rarely leave to integrate into the Malaysian society. My Berea College professor somehow knew that rare person who grew up in Iban tribe and decided to leave and move to Kuala Lumpur.

We were also lucky that our visit fell on the week of their Harvest Festival. That was the week when they do allow visitors into their village because of their belief that the more food that gets eaten during the Harvest Festival, the more plentiful the harvest will be the following year. The trip up to the remote village could only be taken by these special trucks because of the steep mountain they had to drive up. The trucks had nets attached to it in the bed of the truck and that's all we had to hang on to so that we did not fall out of them during the ascent. Iban tribes live in these long houses that have the main level with a balcony and then each family had their own entrance into their private apartment, and you could walk downstairs for more rooms.

When we entered, we were greeted by the entire tribe dressed in their traditional outfits. They were playing drums and women were handing us rice wine as a welcome drink. To show us the importance of our visit, the tribe slaughtered a huge pig right in front of our eyes. As you can imagine, a lot of American girls on this trip started crying when they saw this. This was a normal thing for me as I grew up around animal sacrifices in church, which I will describe later. After this ceremony, we were asked to sit on the balcony of the long house for blessings. Their shaman was wearing a hat with many feathers attached to it and as he was reciting his blessings, he would interrupt them by making loud bird noises. I was startled the first time he did that.

After the blessings, food arrived. We were all given plates and then women would walk around and put food on our plates. We were told that no matter what, we absolutely had to eat everything on our plate. No food can be wasted. This is a tough situation to be in when the tribe members want you to eat as much as possible because they believe they will have a more plentiful harvest after that. Eventually we literally had to hover over our plates to cover them and not let them put any more food on them. Some of the highlights of the menu where fried bats on skewers, pig fat (literal fat with no meat on it) and white pudding that would just stick to the roof of your mouth until you used your fingers to get it off. We ate it all.

There was no running water or typical toilets. You just had to squat over the hole to do your business. However, all Iban men did not bother with that. They would just urinate off the balcony when they had to go. I accidentally saw more penises in three days that we stayed there that I care to admit. Lots of drinking was involved as well. When the tribe got drunk, they wanted some entertainment. Their entertainment entailed a wrestling match, men trying to get coins out of bowls filled with flour with their mouths only and karaoke. Drunk people singing karaoke for hours as you try to fall asleep would be one of the rooms in hell if you ask me. By sunrise, everyone finally went to bed, and we were able to sleep on the thin mattresses they laid for us on the balcony. We had mosquito nets covering us as we slept. The next morning, I woke up because I felt something crawling on my face. It was the biggest cockroach I have ever seen in my life. I jumped and screamed in disgust!

In general, all bugs are oversized in Malaysia. They have the biggest moths I have ever seen in my life. One of the interesting things I witnessed was a father who caught a moth, tore off its wings and gave the body to his toddler to play with as it could not fly away anymore. Their kids did not have any actual toys, so they played with what was available to them. I was ready to go home after the first day, but we had two more days of these festivities.

An interesting aspect of their culture is that they feed guests first, then men, then women and children last. I asked why this order? Apparently, they believe that they need to feed their providers first to ensure the survival of the tribe. I have been to over 30 countries since this trip and I've yet to experience a culture that was so different from my own.

Finding Courage to Change

Chapter 7:

Wrong Love Choices

The common theme of my dating life is that I created illusions in my head about the man I was seeing. Because of my desire to connect, I tended to ignore their downsides and projected onto them a better personality and traits than they really had. I never had a healthy role model of what a man should be like or what a healthy loving relationship looks like when I was growing up. So, I was left to figure out everything on my own and learn on my own mistakes. I had to become self-reliant in response to feeling abandoned and betrayed by my family. I got so used to feeling emotionally alone in my own family that I did not expect anything different from a relationship. I was taught that I could only be loved when I was bringing value. I have never experienced unconditional love.

The most destructive relationship I've ever been in was right after my first love. My heart was still in shattered pieces after my first boyfriend and I broke up when Luke appeared in my life. He was an exchange student in the same program as me just a few years older and we met at one of the alumni gatherings. He was handsome, confident but borderline cocky. His blue eyes just pierced you when he looked at you. He told me a compliment that sparked something in me and asked for my number. Our romance was fast and furious. He used my insecurities and broken heart to make me feel like I was not worthy of having him as my boyfriend. He hid our relationship from our common acquaintances. My brain and my self-worth would completely shut down around him. I forgave his cheating incident and his constant negative comments about my appearance. I went down to size 4 in attempt to please him. I would leave my house at night, risking my safety while taking public transportation just to see him for an hour. He would push me to the edge where I would break up with him only to have him lure me right back. I was anxious and neurotic. I put him on a pedestal, and I was worshiping him. It was the kind of love that would absolutely destroy me if I did not leave. I knew the only way for me to escape him was to leave the country. That relationship was one other major motivator for me to come back to the US. It took me a while to get over him as he would constantly try to reappear in my life through social media even after both of us were already married.

During my sabbatical in May of 2022, I was a week away from going back to the US from Georgia when Luke reached out to me after many years asking for a meeting. It had been almost 15 years since we broke up. This time my response to his attempt to reach out was not anger or just ignoring him. This time I agreed to a meeting.

I set up a meeting in the hotel restaurant where my close friend was the manager. I knew she would be working that afternoon and asked her to get me at exactly 4 pm. That would give Luke only one hour and then I had an escape route. I got physically sick an hour before our meeting and almost cancelled it all together. However, when he walked in, I saw a middle-aged man with a belly and wrinkles and the demeanor that was nothing like the Luke that I remembered. I had no clue what he wanted to discuss so I just asked him how he was. This opened up 30 minutes of him talking about his job and the house that he renovated and his two daughters. He was living an ordinary life.

As he talked, I thought: "Thank you God for not allowing me to marry this man." Then I told him about my life and everything I was doing. I was getting really bored with this conversation and was already thinking if our hour was up. He probably noticed and asked for a check and said that he had to go back to work.

As I walked out of that meeting heading toward my hotel, I had no clue why Luke wanted to see me, but I realized how much I needed this meeting. I realized that I placed this man on the pedestal in my youth and he was still there until that day when we met. I realized how much insecurity left from this relationship was deep inside me that had just disappeared after this meeting. I felt lighter as I walked down the street. This man and the relationship no longer had any pull on me. What an ordinary life I would have lived and how many experiences I would have missed out on if I would have intertwined my life with this man. I am thankful for the opportunity to have closure. I know many people do not get to do that. I was grateful that I left the country to start my new life in the US back in 2008.

I met my now ex-husband, John, in 2009 at Berea college and we started dating shortly after. He was a local Kentucky boy with a gentle heart. I think subconsciously I was looking to find the polar opposite personality of my father and John fulfilled that image for me. He was kind, child-like and he loved me. We got married in 2011. John got baptized in the Orthodox Church so that he could marry me in church in Georgia. I've always dreamed of getting married in Svetitskhoveli church because it is the oldest and most prominent church in Georgia. On our wedding day, when we walked into Svetitskhoveli about to have our ceremony and the priest saw us, he turned to me and with disgust in his face said: "You could not find anyone better to marry?" You see, my husband-to-be was half black, half white and we had a case of a racist priest. I was so thankful that John did not understand Georgian language and he did not experience the pain of being discriminated against on his wedding day. I felt so hurt and in disbelief that a servant of God could say such a painful statement. The whole ceremony was just a blur as I was fighting back tears.

Marriage was not a smooth ride as our personalities were not a good match and we were too young to work out our own issues to build a healthy relationship. Now, I recognize that I was so broken that I could not make him feel loved the way he needed it. In return, he acted out in various ways such as poor eating habits or buying things he did not really need. By the time we divorced in 2015, I was 30 pounds heavier and had $25000 in credit card debt. When issues began, I did not give up on our marriage without a fight though. We started going to couple's counseling to work on issues in our marriage.

During one of these counseling sessions when we were sitting in the reception area and John suddenly burst into tears and admitted that he cheated on me with someone the previous weekend. I have always believed in trusting your partner and had no problem with my husband going to an overnight party at his friend's farmhouse. I didn't enjoy those parties and didn't feel like going that particular weekend. I also didn't believe that I should prevent an adult from doing something that they wanted and had no problem with my husband going by himself. When he told me about his cheating incident, I knew I could never forgive unfaithfulness and our marriage was over. I left my marriage with 2 suitcases, a blow-up mattress, 2009 Nissan Altima, massive credit card debt and a broken heart.

I was lucky that in 2012 I met my friend, Katie, while I was pursuing my MBA at the University of Kentucky. We bonded over radishes. One day I walked into a classroom, and I saw Katie eating cut up radishes with salt. I told her that I had never seen anyone else in the US eat radishes like this and that is exactly how I love to eat them as well. We laughed and began getting to know each other better that day. We grew closer as friends and Katie was my safe heaven as I left my marriage. I had no money, no job, no place to stay. I am not sure where I would have been during that time if not for her. We always joke that the best thing we got out of our MBA was each other.

Both Katie and I started working for her stepfather's company as sales executives in different markets. She lived in Cincinnati, and I lived in Louisville. During this time, I made a mistake that many people make after exiting a painful relationship or marriage. I decided that I did not want anything serious, and I was just going to have fun and explore. That's when I met Matt. I knew right away that he was not someone I would ever want to date seriously but our chemistry was off the charts, and we had a lot of fun hanging out together. This is the period of my life I am least proud of. I drank too much and partied too much.

After my divorce I did not want to date anyone seriously for a while until I met Andrew. He made his career after he moved to Italy from Greece and got transferred to the US to start up the US branch of an Italian company he worked for. We met in Kentucky and our relationship lasted 2.5 years. I believe that we were a good match and we truly loved each other. Timing of when we met and how our relationship was built was wrong though. We met during Andrew's first week in the US and we spent every day together until he had to go back to Italy. Being apart but talking almost daily helped us to get to know each other and create intimacy. When he got back to the US, we had an amazing two months until we learned that his US branch would be relocating from KY to Atlanta, Georgia. On the surface, everything was going great between us. The reality was that our roles in our relationship were not positioned correctly. Because Andrew was new to the US, I had to take a role of a protector for him and us as a couple. I had to teach him how things operated and often it was easier for me to take care of business on his behalf.

This immediately created a relationship where my masculine energy was rising and his was lowering. We were a good match though and this imbalance was hidden from us for a long time. We commuted every weekend to see each other for six months once Andrew relocated to Atlanta while I remained in Kentucky. Looking back, I can't believe that I was driving 7 hours each way every other weekend to spend a day and a half with Andrew. Our love was giving us the energy to do it. Then the company I worked for got sold to a corporation and all of us at the top level were laid off. This event gave us an opportunity to finally be in the same city. I packed up my house and moved down to Atlanta two weeks after my lay off.

I found another job within a month in Atlanta and began a new chapter. I wanted to do things differently this time around. I realized that I had lived for almost 10 years in Kentucky and had not created a community or had many friends. I was so caught up in climbing that corporate ladder, that it didn't leave any time for socializing. It's a miracle that I was able to build a relationship with Andrew during this period.

I decided that I would put in an effort to build a community around me in my new hometown. Frankly, Atlanta is the first place I have ever lived where it felt like home to me. This is probably why I finally decided to purchase a house instead of renting it. Before Atlanta, I had been moving every single year to a new place. I never threw out cardboard boxes because I knew I would be packing again in 12 months. It was the most amazing feeling to finally be able to get rid of the boxes. Andrew and I created a wonderful friend group and we loved to host. To everyone we were the ideal couple.

Our relationship started to crack for me when I had my first health scare. After my annual pap test, abnormal cells were discovered in my cervix. The gynecologist I saw recommended surgery where part of my cervix would be removed to make sure that those abnormal cells did not become cancerous. I had never had health issues before that and I fell apart for the first time in my life. I did not know what to do and I was extremely distraught. It did not help that I received weekly calls from my gynecologist asking if I was ready to schedule the surgery.

In that moment, the extent of Andrew's support was verbal affirmation that everything would be okay. What I needed in that moment was the partner who would step up to some action. Eventually, I had to pull myself together, find the best gynecologist in town and get a second opinion with her. I was so lucky that this doctor accepted me as a new patient because she spared me the surgery by using a new non-invasive procedure out of Europe that had 95% success rate in removing abnormal cells from the cervix.

This was a pivotal point in our relationship for me because it opened my eyes to the dynamic we had been having. All major decisions for both of us were made by me. All vacations were planned by me. All social events were organized by me, etc. Andrew took a secondary role in the relationship, and I was pulling both of us forward. I realized that I would never feel secure enough with this man to have children with him. Then I saw that he was shopping for engagement rings. I knew I would not be able to say yes to his proposal and I ended our relationship before he would ask me to marry him.

The response that Andrew had is a common response that men have during break ups like this one. "But I thought you liked doing all these things yourself, so I let you." There is no regret about anything now, but I have wondered if things would have been different between us if we established the correct masculine/feminine dynamic in our relationship from the get-go. The answer is maybe. I cannot have a definitive answer either way. I just know that this was the toughest break up because there was no anger between us. Just the realization that we could not proceed forward as a married couple. He has gotten married since then and I truly wish for happiness and marital bliss for the family that he created as he is a wonderful man.

My next significant learning experience was with Carlos. On the surface, my experience with Carlos looks like it was written for the best Hollywood romance movie. We met on a dating app and chatted for a while before we met in real life. We then planned our first date. He arrived at our first date with a dozen red roses for me. That's not very common now, so one extra point goes to Carlos for that gesture. The second date went very well. A few days after our second date I went on my annual beach trip with friends. He stayed in touch via text and was very interested in everything I had going on during my trip. One day he asked where I was going for dinner that day. I told him and didn't think anything of it until the restaurant manager presented me with a dozen red roses at dinner.

The manager said those were sent for me. I, of course, immediately texted Carlos and thanked him for this romantic gesture. Then he told me that he had another surprise for me. He said: "After you are done with dinner, walk over to the ice cream shop around the corner and get some ice cream for you and your girlfriend on me." I thought that was very sweet and thoughtful. We walked to the ice cream shop and got our ice cream as planned and then as I walk outside of the shop, who do I see sitting outside waiting for me? You guessed it right, it was Carlos himself. He drove 7 hours from Atlanta to take me out for ice cream.

After a while, we dropped my friend at the hotel and went to a bar to get a drink just Carlos and me. My old self would have been swept off her feet for this gesture. My new self felt a little like he was crossing a boundary. I made sure he knew this gesture did not mean I would be having sex with him that night. He dropped me off at my hotel room and then he drove back to Atlanta. Then when I was back in Atlanta, he called me and asked what I was doing. I had a rough day at work that day and was craving a burger, which never happens by the way. So, I was on the way to my favorite restaurant to get a burger and a glass of red wine. He told me that I should not be doing that and should have a salad instead so that I could work on having a J LO body. That was the last time we spoke as I told him last thing I need in my life is a man telling what I can and cannot eat.

His pattern of behavior got me very curious and caused me to do some research about it. My suspicions were confirmed that this was a case of a narcissist. Narcissists are the type of men or women who do these kinds of grand gestures to make an impression on their date. However, they do it more for themselves because it showcases them as someone unique. They blossom in looking back at amazing things they have done to capture their date's interest. The flipside of the coin of that is that they have a certain image of how their partner should look and behave. If you do not fit that image, it will be voiced immediately. I brought this example to hopefully help someone else to not be blinded by the dust that narcissists throw into your eyes when they first start dating you.

My pattern of idealizing the man I was with would work for a period of time. Eventually problems would arise, but I felt so dedicated to making each relationship work until I could not anymore. Sooner or later, the pink sunglasses came off, the illusions would shatter, and I was left with the reality that I had chosen the wrong partner for myself...yet again.

Then, I would take some time to myself to heal and grow and would start the dating process over.

I realized that I put pressure on myself to stay and work through the problems in the relationship because I believed that if I could just fix those problems, things would improve. But here is the truth - I am not going to be rescued by a partner and when I choose a wrong partner, my life is not going to improve either. I had to grow through these relationship lessons so that I could find wholeness inside of myself, independent of the relationship. I can no longer base my happiness on my partner, nor can I continue feeling incomplete without a partner. I had to learn to love myself unconditionally through the unconditional love I receive from my relationship with God. I had to learn that I am worthy to be loved just for who I am - not for the value I bring to the relationship or how convenient I make the life for my partner. I spent time alone to embrace this independent part of me and learn to be happy on my own. I learned to feel truly authentic, aligned, and content with who I am.

Here is an interesting thing that happened once this shift has occurred within me. I no longer needed to be on any dating apps because I was like honey attracting bees. High value men have started popping up left and right asking me out on a date. I no longer had to worry about basic things on my check list as every eligible bachelor crossing my path was handsome, successful, smart, funny, etc. I was focusing on how I felt around them and how they treated me. I also was asking myself the same question after every date: "Would I want to spend the rest of my life with this man?" If the answer was yes or maybe, I would continue getting to know them. However, as soon as the answer was no, I would politely end the courtship. I no longer let myself be rushed or worry about committing to quickly in fear of missing out on this next great dating opportunity. It takes patience to discover what's truly best for me. Finding the right partner in life is not something to be rushed or taken lightly.

Chapter 8:

How I Found God in the Pandemic

I was blessed a second time in my life to be matched with an amazing host family in Berea. I did not realize until 12 years later what a gift God had given me and why he brought us together. Back then I was not a believer, and my host father was a pastor and my host mother worked for an organization that organized mission trips around the world. Any attempt from their side to talk about faith was shut down from my side but they were patient and loving with me and never pushed me. Now I can admit that I was angry with God because I felt that it was unfair that He let me go through all those terrible experiences as a child. If He was the God of Love, then why did He not love me enough to prevent all those traumatic events from happening? As I refused God, my host family loved me as I was, and our friendship was blossoming as time passed and through changes in everyone's' lives.

Fast-forward to 2020 and that fateful Pandemic that we all went through, and things shifted supernaturally for me.

It was October 2020 and that fateful night I woke up at 3 a.m. unexpectedly. I felt fully awake - as if I slept through the entire night. My mind was sharp and body well rested. I do not have a logical reason why I decided to pray then. I've never prayed in my entire life and nothing particularly stressful or upsetting happened that week to justify my desire to pray. Yet, there I was lying in bed and asking God to reveal my purpose in life and show me the path that I was meant to take. To my surprise, I heard a voice that gave specific directions on what I needed to do in the morning.

As I was laying in bed in shock, processing what just had happened, I wondered if I had dreamed it or imagined it. My logical brain analyzed the situation quickly and determined that I was wide awake when it happened and that I did not imagine it. Confused, I decided to go back to sleep and ponder on this some more in the morning. The next morning when I woke up, I did not go to work. Instead, I went to the grocery store and bought the items on the list given to me by the voice I heard. As a result, I made exactly twenty-four lunch bags. I packed them in my car and headed to downtown Atlanta as I had seen people struggling with homelessness hang out in that part of town.

As I drove around, I would pull over when I saw a person in need and ask them if they wanted some lunch. After about an hour of driving around and passing out lunches, I saw a group of people struggling with homelessness hanging out together. I counted how many they were, and I had the exact number of lunches left. I parked my car and grabbed all the lunch bags and walked over. They were happy to take food and as I had no more food to give out, I proceeded to walk over to my car to go home. I thought: "I fulfilled my instructions, so I am done!" Before I reached my car, I heard one of the women call me to come over to her. I walked back to see what she needed. She told me that she had a gift for me that she wanted me to take. She gave me a small bird made from clay and on that bird, there was a phrase written - "Now in God's Hands." When I saw that, I thanked her quickly and turned around because I could feel tears coming and I did not want her to see me crying. I quickly got into my car and closed my eyes. I knew then that the voice I heard was from God and I was called to be in God's hands. I accepted Jesus Christ as my Savior in that moment. My life was forever changed then.

I started studying the Bible and learning what it meant to be a Christian. The following August, I was called and felt ready to be baptized. My host father was the one who baptized me and it was truly a celebration for us. My host family had been praying for me to find God for over ten years and finally their prayers had been answered. It was an emotional ceremony that brought us so much closer together. Until I found my faith, I did not even realize that there was this invisible wall that I put up and separated myself from them. Suddenly that wall was shattered, and I felt the love like I never felt before.

The unfortunate side of this story is that Believer's Baptism is not something that ever takes place in Orthodox Christianity. Therefore, my mother believed that I had joined a cult. Orthodox Christianity still follows a lot of traditions that come from the Old Testament. I grew up with the tradition of animal sacrifices. It always felt very transactional to me. The way it worked in my family was - my father or grandmother would ask God for something and as a way to thank Him, they would purchase a lamb for sacrifice.

One church in my hometown would conduct these ceremonies. So, we would get into a car and drive up the mountain toward this church up until a certain point. At a specific marking, we would all get out of the car and would walk up to the church. The belief was if the lamb would run up toward the church instead of you dragging it behind you, that means that God accepts your sacrifice. Then the priests would conduct the sacrifice ceremony and would call you when it was done. Only a specific dish was allowed to be prepared with this meat and you were not allowed to take any leftovers home after you were done feasting.

This whole ceremony felt wrong to me as a child, and I always wondered if it was just an excuse for feasting and getting drunk which would inevitably happen after each ceremony.

Once I came to my faith, I also realized that I had an encounter with the Holy Spirit earlier in my life, but I did not realize what it was then. I have very few memories that are crystal clear as if they happened yesterday. Most of my memories are blurry and difficult to recall. In this memory, I remember the crisp fall weather, the cracks in the asphalt in my school's courtyard and even the coat I was wearing. Every detail is bright and vivid in my memory. I came out of the school building during a break only to look around me and have an odd thought cross my mind: "You are meant for more than this life." This was a defining moment in my life that ignited the fire in my soul that pushed me forward in my life. I always thought it was my own thought until three years ago when I realized that it was God speaking to me. Wording in this story is extremely important. The thought was "You" and not "I". I don't know about you but when I speak about myself in my head, I don't talk in third person. This was a circumstance when I did and that tells me that Someone else planted that thought and it grew stronger and stronger each day. Have you had a defining moment like this in your life?

Chapter 9:

Starting the Healing Journey

As an immigrant to the US, the biggest American dream I had was to buy a condo in a high rise building and be in the middle of action overseeing the skyscrapers around me. I accomplished this dream on March 2nd, 2020. I was not fully satisfied with the look of my newly acquired home, and I decided to renovate it completely to fit my taste. As we all know from history, the famous Covid-19 shut down then happened all over the US. The crippling fear that I made the biggest mistake of my life had to be pushed down because I had no other choice but to move forward. At that point, my condo was in the demolishment stage and unlivable, thus I had to push forward and finish the renovations. By the grace of God, everything was completed within one month and I finally moved into my dream home. My excitement and happiness lasted exactly one month. Then I remember sitting on my couch and thinking: "Now what?" This house has not brought me the fulfillment and contentment that I was seeking in life. What was I missing? Have you ever experienced something like this in your life?

During this period, I was among the numerous workaholics who were forced to slow down by the pandemic. I went from having a crazy schedule of 12-hour workdays outside of my home and plans every weekend to working from home every day and only going out for groceries. Magically, my work was getting done in almost half the time with all the meetings happening online. Yet, I continued hitting my sales numbers every month. With so much free time on my hands, I decided it was time for me to seek additional therapy to work through my childhood trauma. After numerous failed relationships and dating trials, I realized that I was the common denominator. I knew that if I wanted to get off this merry-go-round, I had to do something drastic to change my pattern of behavior. I decided that regular therapy is not going to cut it as I had five years of it in my twenties. While it definitely helped me get through the worst triggers and move past some things from my childhood, I knew more work needed to be done. I was seeking a hypnotherapist in the Atlanta area. I was lucky to have found an amazing one.

If you have done regular therapy in your life, you know that it takes several sessions for your therapist to get to know your story and to actually begin the therapy process. You move slowly and sometimes it can feel like you are not making any progress at all. This was certainly not my experience with my hypnotherapist, Dana. About 15 minutes into our first session, she already figured out the reason why I had three failed long-term relationships and why I kept attracting the same type of a man. In a nutshell, because of the way I was raised and conditioned, I was fulfilling a role of a protector and provider for my family. At that point in time, neither my mother nor my brother was working and I had been fully supporting them for the past eight years.

I was always solving their problems and keeping their lifestyle afloat for them. I was also an "emotional toilet" for my mother where she got to dump all her negativity into and then I had to resolve it on my own. I was raised by my family in the way where I believed that I could only be loved if I was useful and doing things for my loved ones. Thus, every day, I had to put on my "armor" and go fight the world alone while my family depended on me for everything.

I remember hearing on a TV show a psychologist talk about our "armor" in terms of color and it definitely clicked for me. I wish I remembered psychologist's name and exact wording to quote here but I will do my best to relay the point she was making.

Imagine that through your childhood experiences, past relationships, culture, religion, etc., you have built an armor and this armor that you put on every day has a color - red. So, you go out into the world with this color red and therefore, you attract mates who are attracted to color red. However, in reality, your true color is purple, and you are this completely different person on the inside. However, the person you are trying to attract to the purple color never actually sees that color on the outside, and therefore you never end up attracting them. This was such an aha moment for me. I realized that I have built this persona of a go-getter, successful businesswoman who takes care of everything and that was what was seen on the outside. I kept attracting men who were attracted to those type of women. However, I was seeking someone different. I was seeking someone who would be attracted to my true inner gentler self.

The scary realization was that I actually did not know exactly who I was once I shed this outer layer. I needed to seek my inner child to heal her so that the adult me could shine through without all that baggage.

Dana also told me that I will never want to have children either until I stop playing this role of protector and provider. Psychologically, I already have two children depending on me for everything. Dana proceeded to draw on the board the correct order of priorities for women and men when feminine and masculine energies are in balance. My priorities were definitely out of whack, as I followed more of a man's priority order. One thing that did not click in either men or women category for me is that she put God as number one priority for both. This was before I found God.

I was still very angry with God. I could never understand why he would allow so many horrific painful experiences to happen to me as I was an innocent child. This is a very common response to trauma. First, you go through denial and then through anger before you move to healing. I was stuck in this anger stage for many years without even realizing it. Also, I grew up in Orthodox Christianity where a lot of rules and customs did not make sense to me at all. For example, as a woman you are not allowed to enter church if you are menstruating. I always wondered: "If God created women to have a menstruation and God always wants us to enter His house to worship, why would he prevent women from doing so while we are doing something so natural and that is connected to us continuing mankind?" So, I had a lot of questions and concerns in addition to my anger. I felt that I was treated unfairly by God. Fast forward to my session with Dana and she told me, my prioritization in life is wrong and God is first. I definitely had some resentful feelings as I listened to her. But I kept those feelings to myself at that point.

Then we continued to have our first session of hypnosis. Now, do not imagine hypnotherapy as what you see in those Las Vegas shows where people are made to make sounds as chickens to get laughs out of the audience. During hypnotherapy, you actually remember everything, but the therapist helps you enter your own subconscious, and you cannot really control where within your memories and subconscious you are going to end up. During my first session, I saw myself within my mother's womb. And then I had a flash of when in her pregnancy she was, and I knew that at that moment she was about 7 months pregnant. Now that blows my mind that within our subconscious, we have hidden memories as early as before we were even born! I also learned that instead of blissfulness, even then I felt my mother's anxiety. I did not feel protected even as a fetus. This has a significant impact on how I view time of pregnancy now. Beyond the nutrients and vitamins, having a calm and happy mother-to-be is just as important for the development of the child in a mother's womb.

It makes sense to me now why I experienced anxiety even in my mother's womb. As I wrote earlier, my mother escaped my overprotective grandmother and into the arms of my father as soon as she graduated high school.

My experience of seeing myself in the womb during the hypnotherapy was explained by Dana to be quite rare and it meant that my subconscious was preparing me for quite a journey ahead. I was told to buckle up. Nothing could have prepared me for what was ahead. Throughout this type of therapy, you are taught to stop suppressing your true feelings. I did not know there were so many ways that I wanted to hurt my parents, but I allowed all of this to unravel in my subconscious. During therapy, in my mind, I have thrown my father from the balcony, burnt him, stabbed him with a knife to name a few of my experiences. At the end of this therapy, I finally could say that I have moved past the anger stage in my healing process. However, I knew that I needed to push myself further and move toward forgiveness.

Finding Courage to Change

Chapter 10:

News That Altered the Trajectory of My

Life

It was providential when I decided to take that specific Monday off work. I had no explainable reason for it. I just could not force myself to even think about going to work the following morning. It was weird that I felt this way because I had just gotten back from a month-long vacation in Europe less than two weeks earlier. However, on Sunday night I submitted a request for PTO for January 31st, 2022, the next day. I woke up that fateful Monday morning to see my Facebook Messenger app blown up with messages from my Godmother, Nino. It is amazing how technology could carry news that forever would alter the trajectory of that year and eventually my entire life.

I clicked the link to view what was causing such a commotion, and nothing could have prepared me for what I was about to see. It was horrific news articles about my own family being in the spotlight of the Georgian media. And by

Georgia, I mean the country in Eastern Europe where I am from, not the state, Georgia, in the United States where I currently reside.

From the cold voice of the news broadcaster announcing the news, I learned that the night before, my 82-year-old grandfather stabbed his own son, my uncle, 30 times while my uncle was asleep. Afterwards, my grandfather proceeded to his neighbors' apartment to tell them what he had just done and asked them to call the ambulance. He also said out loud that he hoped that he killed his son. In absolute disbelief, I was staring at images of the balcony where I stood so many times as a child. I saw the knife used during stabbing-the same knife my grandfather used to cook meals for us.

Then, I absolutely lost my composure when they showed the video of my grandfather. He looked so frail and was barely able to walk on his own as he was led in handcuffs by the police. My grandfather had been in an accident where he broke his leg many years ago and it never properly healed. As long as I remember him, he always walked with a limp and with an assistance of a cane. I watched the short clip while sobbing as he was led by the police walking with difficulty into the building. The feeling of grief and insufferable pity came upon me like a big ocean wave.

By this point in time of my life, I had not spoken to anybody from my father's side of the family for fourteen years. I wondered what kind of a life my grandfather must have been living, that taking such a sin upon his soul and killing his own son was a better solution and outcome than continuing his life as it was. There must have been a sense of desperation he felt to be able to take that step. Killing another human is a hard step to take for the majority of people and this was a situation of taking a life of your own flesh and blood. I also wondered if my grandfather's mental state had just snapped and it will be the regret he will carry for the remainder of his life. So many unanswered questions.

Then more videos from social media poured in. In one of the interviews my grandfather was describing how my uncle used to abuse him in a drunken rage. As he was talking, during the police questioning, my grandfather showed a big scar on his head. I kept wondering what happened to my little 9-year-old cousin. I never met him as I was already living in the US by the time he was born, but I knew through common acquaintances that his mother had left the country and was working in Italy and my grandfather was my cousin's true caretaker. So, what was going to happen to this small child now?

His father was in the intensive care unit of the hospital fighting for his life and his grandfather was in jail. He was left alone at nine years old, not knowing what was happening. I found out from friends I knew who still lived in Gori, that the neighbors told my cousin that both his father and grandfather were sick with Covid-19 and had to be quarantined. I cannot blame them for the lie. After all, how do you tell a child that his world would never be the same and people who are supposed to love and protect him would hurt him in such an unimaginable way? I was praying that night for my cousin's mother to come back to Georgia to take him with her to Italy.

Deep inside I knew that if no one from my family would step up to take care of this child, I would not be able to walk away and abandon this innocent kid. I would not let him go live in an orphanage. I guess there is some truth to the expression: "Blood is thicker than water". Here I was contemplating how I would need to step up my life for a child I never even met, but who was related to me. Truth be told, I was relieved to find out that his mother did come back to attend the funeral as my uncle passed away 9 days after the stabbing incident. She took my cousin with her to Italy, so I did not have to make this life-altering decision after all. My grandfather passed away while in prison a year later from complications caused by Covid-19.

My family in this heart-breaking story is an example of generations upon generations of abusive parents all over the world who end up raising abusive children. This pattern of behavior culminated in this tragedy that transpired between father and son in my family. I kept thinking: "What is the higher purpose of this situation? Will this tragedy finally break the cycle of violence in my family?" I had to move across the world to escape this part of my life, but will this wake up my family members who remained in Georgia? I don't have the answers to these questions yet and I might never get these answers. Well, at least, not in this life.

That entire day when I first learned about this tragedy, I would sporadically burst into tears. I felt such grief and helplessness. In situations like this, it is typical for us, humans, to ask ourselves what we could have done to prevent this or that tragedy from happening and I was no exception. I was also hoping that my mother would reach out to me in support but that never happened. At that point in time, it had been two years since we had cut ties and stopped communicating. Through my hypnotherapy, I had realized that I was stuck in an unhealthy pattern with my mother that I will unpack here.

My mother has lived in a role of a victim her entire life. It became part of her identity. I was raised to become her confidant, protector, and supporter. The role that I did not even realize was forced upon me until I was in my thirties. My mother finally decided to divorce my father after I had shaken her world by leaving Georgia to move to the United States as a student. Suddenly, the only person she could rely on was gone and that has shaken her to the core. She did not know how to deal with the wave of the depression that hit her. She escaped her reality by playing video games all evening after she got home from work.

This behavior has disrupted the abuser-victim roles my father and mother had been playing for twenty years. She no longer cared how much he drank or if he wanted to fake kill himself. Her indifference enraged my father one night and in a drunken state, he almost killed my mother when he threw her against the mirror breaking it in half and leaving her with a scar the length of her spine. As she was bleeding on the ground, crying from pain, my elderly grandmother came out to scream at my father. My father kicked my grandmother in the stomach and then left. That night was the final straw for my mother. She called the police for the first time in her twenty years of being abused and my father was taken to jail. She changed the locks on the entrance door and kicked my father out of the house. As expected, my father did not like his life being disrupted and he harassed my mother for months until my mother finally hired a lawyer and began divorce proceedings. That was the wakeup call for my father when he realized that his life as he knew it was over.

This event pushed my protective instincts toward my mother over the edge. There were unspoken expectations that I would call my mother almost every day so she wouldn't feel lonely. Our conversations were mostly about how difficult her life was and what I could do to make it better. There was also a narcissistic trait of living vicariously through me. The concept of "Mother-Queen" was very much alive underneath it all. She sought attention where she could find it.

With her friends, she always acted arrogantly when the conversation was about their children as I was the most successful one and she truly believed that it was her achievement. She slowly began alienating people around her because she somehow felt like she was better than them and that allowed her to treat them poorly.

I did not notice any of these patterns of behavior in my twenties as I was suddenly expected to financially support her and my brother once I graduated from my MBA program. I always felt obligated to shield her from my own struggles. I graduated from my MBA program in 2013 when the economy was still not fully recovered after the 2008 recession. My first job had an annual salary of $45,000. During that time, I was also paying off all the credit card debt that my ex-husband left me with, so my monthly income would not allow me to even have internet services the first couple of months after starting my job. I hated the feeling of uncertainty I constantly felt as I never knew if I would have enough money every month to cover my own expenses. I was then also expected to cover my mother's expenses. What was interesting about this relationship was that my mother never actually asked for any money. She used manipulation to ensure that I felt a sense of obligation to make sure she was taken care of. Suddenly, my mother has found a sense of security that she never felt in her marriage by putting this responsibility on my shoulders.

I discovered these patterns after years of therapy. I finally sat my mother and my brother down in front of the video call. I said: "You always tell me that you want me to be happy and build a family of my own. I am not going to be able to do that until I stop playing the role of a protector and provider for you two. Therefore, I need you to get jobs and stop being reliant on me financially. I also need you to stop dumping all of your negativity on me as I no longer can play a psychologist role for you either. I have done everything I could by helping you buy an apartment in Tbilisi. You have more opportunities there. I have paid off all your debt as well and I have paid for my brother's education." My mother seemed to be supportive at first and immediately went out to get a job. My brother, on the other hand, immediately stopped talking to me.

A couple of weeks went by and my mother kept complaining about how cold the space where she worked was or how long it took her to walk home at night after work. Subconsciously she was trying to make me feel guilty for forcing her to get a job. When I asked her to stop sharing these negative thoughts with me, she snapped telling me that she would die under the bridge before she would ask for my help again. I finally snapped and asked her to take responsibility over her own life and over the role she played in her children's traumas before she would contact me again. Our communication ceased in October of 2020 and did not resume until Easter of 2023, when we had our first phone call. It was the first healthy conversation I have ever had with my mother.

Through my sabbatical I worked hard to find forgiveness toward my mother and writing this book was the healing balm that I needed to reach peace and forgiveness. We finally found our path back toward each other but this time our relationship is structured in a healthy way where she is a mother, and I am her child. We had to break down completely so that we could start rebuilding our relationship in a new way now.

Finding Courage to Change

Chapter 11:

Shedding the Old Life

Going back to the day of my grandfather stabbing my uncle, I remember that I felt very alone in my grief when my mother did not reach out to me even after such a tragic development.

That afternoon, I mustered up enough energy to call the owner of the company I was working for. At that time, I was working as a Sales Executive and had been bringing in close to 45% of the revenue for this company quite successfully for 4 years. I told my boss everything that had happened and told him that I was not sure if I would be able to work "business as usual" the following day. His response absolutely killed my faith in corporate America. He told me not to take an official day off but to put in my out-of-office message to say that I was conducting surveys so that I could still be available in case of an emergency. I must add here that we were selling products for construction projects and not selling life-saving medical equipment. Emergencies in my line of work was never life-or-death kind of a situation. I hung up the phone in disbelief. I knew in my heart that if I was in his shoes and my employee would have told me about a situation like the one, I would have told them to take as much time off as they needed. I would have asked if there was anything I could do for them. I would have shown more compassion and understanding to the pain and suffering. I felt this was the wrong way to handle the situation by all accounts.

The very next day on February 1st, 2022, I did not take the day off. Instead, I walked into his office and gave my official 2-week notice. I could not work for the company who showed zero compassion to me any longer than I had to. This was the beginning of my sabbatical.

I had known for a while that I wanted to take some time off to find my purpose and my mission in life. I had hired a career coach a few months earlier who had helped me realize that no amount of money that I was earning at my current job would bring me the fulfillment and joy I was seeking out of work. My coach introduced me to a Japanese concept of Ikegai. It is a term that has no literal translation in the English language, but it is a term that consists of four components and that embodies the idea of happiness in living. You are first asked if you can affirmatively answer the happiness question in all four areas. I was two out of four which confirmed that I needed to make drastic changes in my life.

This is a concept that I now highly recommend to everyone seeking to evaluate their own happiness in life.

For many months, I had been patiently waiting for the right moment to take this big leap. However, what happened in my family and the response I received from my employer significantly expedited my decision to leave my corporate job. No amount of money could have kept me in the environment where there is zero compassion, and I was just someone useful as long as I brought in the sales and made money for the company. I was the top producer in my company, so my employer was not happy with my decision to quit.

My clients were incredibly supportive of my decision, and I received a lot of encouragement from them. Also, I don't think anyone would be happy to say: "Thank God for Covid", but I was beyond happy when I was diagnosed with Covid-19 in those last 2 weeks of my employment, and I did not have to physically go to the office until the last day to turn in my computer.

I expected to feel weird at first and that I would need some time to adjust to the life of not working but let me tell you, that day never came. Quitting my corporate job has been the best decision I could have made in order to find my true authentic self. In fact, sometimes I wonder how I had time to work 12-hour workdays and do things that I loved, spend time with my friends and not be constantly burnt out due to lack of sleep and being overworked. As I am writing this, it's been 11 months since the beginning of my sabbatical, and I do not know what a feeling of boredom is. I have so many things to learn, do, see and people to spend time with. In the past, writing down my story would have felt to be a waste of time but now I feel that it might be one of the more meaningful things I might ever do in my life.

As I started my sabbatical, the end goal was to find my purpose in life. However, I could only see one step at a time of what needed to happen next. That next step was to shed my love of comfort and nice things. That meant downsizing my belongings and selling my beautiful condo. I am extremely blessed to have friends who are happy to support me. My friend, Inna, is one of the top real estate agents in Atlanta. She offered to help me sell my condo at a family and friends' rate. Talk about generosity. My friend, Alina, offered her basement where I could store my belongings and so I did. Now, it's important to mention that until this period of time, I would have never accepted this kind of help from anyone. I always had this feeling of not wanting to inconvenience anyone on one hand and then having a feeling of owing them something in return if someone did something for me, on the other hand. I never allowed my friends a chance to get closer to me through an opportunity to help me when I was in need. However, I was always happy to be the savior and giver type of a friend for my friends. I also felt resentment at times because I felt that I was giving too much and not receiving anything back.

This was a very unfair way of structuring my interactions that I was only able to overcome once I swallowed my pride and admitted that I indeed needed help. I realized that giving with an expectation of receiving something back is not genuine giving. Once I understood my pattern of behavior, I was able to ask myself if I genuinely wanted to help without any expectation of reciprocity in every situation. If the answer was yes, I would proceed. If the answer was no, then it required further evaluation.

The next step was to leave the country and figure out if I wanted to live in the US or somewhere abroad. I packed two suitcases and started my journey on March 15th, 2022. I went to Georgia first. Georgia - my home country in Eastern Europe that is bordered by Russia, Turkey, Armenia, and Azerbaijan. This time I stayed at my Godmother's house instead of renting an apartment like I did last time I was in Georgia. I am so thankful now that I stayed with her. For the first time in my life, I realized what it feels like to be living in a home where there is love and respect and unconditional care. Small acts of care that were probably automatic for my Godmother, were the healing balm for my soul that I needed in that moment. My inner child was receiving the care and love she never received growing up in her own family. This healing was showing in the light I started to shine as an adult.

When I began my journey, I knew that there were 3 things that I wanted to accomplish: go to Israel and visit all the Holy places; do an Ayahuasca retreat in Peru; and go away on a silent retreat. My trip to Israel was a week before Easter. It was the first time I had ever travelled alone to a new country. I learned that I love traveling alone but being part of the tour group. This allowed me to interact with people on daily bases and build meaningful relationships with strangers I encountered along the way. However, when I needed some solitude, I did not have to excuse myself, I could just go.

The journey was not as smooth as I would have hoped for. There was a mistake in the booking for my accommodations and I had to check in and out 3 times in 3 days and move from room to room. I did not feel physically well. What I thought to be allergies ended up being a cold that just would not go away. The realization of what I just had done with my life and the fear of running out of money was running as a constant background noise in my head. I recognized that when the fear alarm goes off in me, that's when I feel far from God. I heard my pastor once say: "Fear and anxiety is an illusion that God is not in charge." I remember and repeat the phrase when anxious thoughts start creeping in. I also had this unrealistic expectation that as soon as I came to Israel, I would immediately feel closer to God. Nothing worthwhile comes easily in life and building faith is no exception.

While in Israel, I often had a reoccurring thought where I would just stop in awe and remember that I was walking in the same places where Jesus once walked. And then I also thought: "How did Jesus survive this intolerable heat with all the walking he had to do and no air conditioning?" I think each Christian must go to Israel at least once in their lifetime and experience this heat to really appreciate the Gospel. When I touched the star that now lays in the place where Jesus was born, I could not hold back my tears. The feeling of connectedness to God felt overwhelming. I felt a step closer to God in that moment. I do admit now that I had these expectations of earth-shattering revelations that would miraculously come to me during this trip that were not fulfilled. However, I did meet an important person who would answer a very important question I had.

When I began my sabbatical, I wondered if I was meant for a life of a "gypsy." I wondered if I could settle in one place but travel all over the world or maybe split my time between various places. I met a woman who did just that for over thirty years. I have asked her many questions about her life and her journey and through these conversations I have understood that I could never live a life like that. I knew that, eventually, I will want to settle down in one place and be part of a community. For this revelation, I am thankful. I also started waking up my dormant ability to dream big. At some point, I just went back to the life of existing and not truly living. I stopped dreaming of the extraordinary things that could happen. When did I lose myself and will I like this new Ana that is emerging? Who am I...truly? It took this drastic change for me to slow down and start down this path of self-discovery.

The next step was my trip to Peru which happened in May of 2022. I had been thinking about doing an Ayahuasca retreat for over four years. Ayahuasca retreats in Peru are an opportunity to experience the traditional shamanic practice of drinking ayahuasca, a powerful Amazonian plant medicine. These retreats are typically several days long and offer an immersive experience, including ayahuasca ceremonies, traditional plant medicine teachings, and personal integration work. Participants can expect to explore the depths of their inner being and to receive healing and insight from the powerful medicine of ayahuasca.

I conducted lots of research about it and worked on myself to be in the right state of mind for it. I felt deep inside that my soul needed something drastic like that to be able to completely let go of my past trauma and move forward as a transformed adult. This is a challenging decision for a Christian because this ceremony does not follow Christian traditions. One of my sisters in Christ even told me that I would be inviting the devil into my life through this ceremony. In the past, I would have been very timid with someone who has been a follower of Christ for many years and either would not have told them about my plan or would have just sat quietly after their comment. However, at that point in my life, I had been praying daily to make sure that this ceremony was something that God was not against. Every time, I would receive the same calm confidence that I needed to proceed with it. Then this thought came after the comment that my friend made about inviting devil into my life: "God used non-believers many times for His purpose in the Bible, and I believe that this shaman is that non-believer in my case." This is a very tough sentence to battle and my friend could not counter it, all she could do is just pray for me as I was embarking on this journey.

Two of my closest girlfriends, Katie and Beth, decided to join me on this journey. After a couple of days of sightseeing in Peru, we finally arrived in Cusco to our retreat center. The owner of the retreat was an inspirational woman with an interesting story that intrigued us. We were supposed to have 3 days of Ayahuasca ceremonies. However, when we arrived, we were told that the shaman had a vision that we should only do two days of Ayahuasca and one day of San Pedro ceremony. We did not know what San Pedro ceremony entailed but decided to go with this new plan. Before Ayahuasca ceremony, you are supposed to fast for at least a week where no alcohol or animal products are consumed to have a much smoother experience. At the retreat center, we were fed a much more conservative diet with a bowl of fruit in the morning and some rice with vegetables in the afternoon. We would not have any other food for the rest of the day.

The first day of our Ayahuasca ceremony began around 6 p.m. We went into a special building built for the ceremony where three mattress beds were waiting for us. Katie took the bed on my right; I was in the middle and Beth was on my left. Our shaman took the time to explain the process of preparing the Ayahuasca root into what they called "medicine of the soul". He explained the effects of it and how he would also be taking it so that he could bring us back if we went too high into our subconsciousness. Because none of us have ever taken any drugs or psychotropics, it was decided that we should take half the dosage that night to see how we would react.

I was praying up until the moment I took the 'medicine' to make sure I was supposed to proceed with this ceremony and never felt otherwise. The typical first sign that the 'medicine' started working is the process of purging. Purging results in violent spurts of vomiting or diarrhea. I am not sure why I was spared this part of the process that night but all I could feel was an absolute sense of tranquility and pure joy. Typical happiness or joy can be described as a burst of hormones causing these heightened feelings in our body and mind that lasts for a short period of time before you return to your baseline. The joy I felt that night was different. The only way I can describe it is that my baseline had lifted. I felt this consistent happiness that lasted for several hours. I also heard this voice that told me that everything that I need to heal is within myself and that I need to stop searching after this trip is completed.

The second day of the ceremony we took a full dosage of the 'medicine'. The way I felt it working was different this night. Suddenly, I felt this wave of energy go through my entire body and my eyes rolled over into my head. I smelled this intense smell of cigarettes mixed with alcohol. It was the smell I tried so hard to forget and block in my memory. Yet, it rushed back with the strength of a tsunami. It was the same smell that my father carried with him each night when he walked into my bedroom to molest me. I started crying like I have never cried before. I was wailing, screaming, and moaning like a wounded animal. I was grieving the death of the little girl inside of me - my childhood that was snatched away from me by my father. The tears that were rolling down my cheeks felt ice cold. My friends came over, hugged me tight and told me how much they loved me. Soon after, there was a light behind my closed eyes that grew brighter and brighter until my tears dried up and I had transitioned into a state of bliss. I also unexpectedly felt complete forgiveness toward my father. This big dark part inside of me just disappeared and I felt lightness in my heart like I've never felt before.

After the healing process that ayahuasca has brought up in regard to my father, came this bliss I felt that is tough to describe. Imagine that every single cell in your body is experiencing an orgasm all at the same time and that would still not give justice to how amazing I felt then. I felt this female energy come over me. It was a power like I had never felt before. For the first time in my life, I was truly proud to be born a woman. I suddenly heard this voice that told me that all my sexual trauma is healed, and I can finally start enjoying sex and having orgasms.

Before this, I had this belief that sex is for men's enjoyment only and that it was something I had to give them. I cared so much about making sure that their male ego was satisfied that I probably could have won an Oscar for my fake orgasm scenes. I did not ask for what I needed or what I wanted. Suddenly, I knew that this was behind me, and I will never fake another orgasm. This is what was happening on the inside, on the outside, apparently, I looked like I was having the most amazing orgasm of my life. I was moaning and arching my back and making all kinds of noises. At some point, the shaman came over and made me sit down and open my eyes. I was so angry with him because I did not want to be back in this reality. Apparently, my subconsciousness was going too high, and I might not have come back if he did not bring me back in that moment. That was a scary thought.

When I calmed down, I sat down with my legs crossed and moved in circles to the sound of the guitar played by the shaman's assistant. Suddenly, I felt someone's arms wrapped around my waist and I felt very calm and secure. Our shaman did not know anything about me or what faith I had or did not have. Suddenly, he came over and told me: "Keep reading your Bible every day like you are now. I see you in Jesus' arms. I was told that you need to read Psalm 91 tomorrow. Make sure you read it." I'd like to believe that the arms I felt were God's hands soothing me and that He used our Shaman to convey this message to me. It reads in Psalm 91 NKJV:

"Surely He shall deliver you from the snare
of the fowler
And from the perilous pestilence.
He shall cover you with His feathers,
And under His wings you shall take refuge;"

I felt protected in that moment when I felt arms around me and now Psalm 91 is what I read when life gets tough and then I remember that I am in Jesus' arms.

The third day was our San Pedro ceremony day. We began early in the morning and joined 6 other women in the same building where our Ayahuasca ceremonies took place. After we took San Pedro medicine, we were told that it is crucial to not throw up for 40 minutes and timer was set. After 40 minutes, each of us was given special sweet herbal tea. This tea would either settle the stomach or would make you vomit, and we were supposed to drink it all and quickly. I proceeded to throw up once I finished this tea. I expected to start feeling physically better, but the relief never came. After about an hour and two cups of tea later, I went up to our shaman and asked her why I kept feeling so nauseous and sick. She told me that I needed to go away and lay down in solitude and ask San Pedro what it was that I was still holding onto.

That is what I did. After a few minutes of laying down, the painful memories from my childhood started flooding into my thoughts. It was the darkest period of my life that I was ashamed of. I carried this shame inside of me for many years. Tears were coming down my face and San Pedro allowed me to finally see that God has forgiven me and to allow myself to forgive myself.

The sense of nausea went away as soon as I was done crying. Next came a vision of me starting an organization that would provide emotional and spiritual healing and a realization that this was my purpose in life.

The most surprising revelation came afterwards. I have always said that I would never have children. I never thought that motherhood was something that I was meant for. I wanted a different life and lifestyle for myself. Despite that, here I was having a vision of giving birth to a child. Tears of joy and love rolling down my face. The voice inside of me was telling me that my child will be the gift to this world. I realized that my childhood traumas that I let go of and the forgiveness I had given myself that day have allowed me to see that I do want to become a mother and have a child. This was a huge shock to my identity. I also could not believe that I was willingly giving up on this big part of my life because of my traumas. It is a scary thought that I might have continued living my life being held back by pain and suffering. I also wonder how many women who refuse to have children might have their trauma holding them back like it was holding me back. I had no clue. I truly thought that this was my own rational decision that I had made for many reasons that I could easily list off. All those reasons no longer felt valid once my trauma was resolved.

Later that evening, we were all sitting by the fire when one of the ladies looks at me and says: "You have healed your heart today, did not you?" I said with a smile on my face: "Yes, I did!" She responded: "Ana, trust yourself more. You have all the answers within you." This experience has brought my confidence back about my decision making. The transformation I have experienced was life changing and I am so grateful.

The final step on my sabbatical's journey was to have a silent retreat. At the beginning, I thought that maybe I would end up going somewhere in India and have a silent yoga and meditation retreat there. However, I learned from a trusted friend about his experience having a silent retreat at the Abbey of Gethsemane- a monastery in the middle of nowhere in Kentucky. I knew in my heart that this is where I was supposed to go. I immediately went to their website- www.monks.org - and got in touch to sign up for their weeklong silent retreat. On September 26th, 2022, I stepped foot on their campus. As soon as you walk in, you are encouraged to completely unplug from the world and to stop talking. Not talking was not the hard part for me, the most difficult part was not having access to my phone. They don't physically take your phone away, of course, but there is no reception inside the monastery. There is Wi-Fi in the library available for several hours during the day if you need it. However, I promised myself that I would not speak or use my cell phone for the entire duration of my stay. There were 36 of us staying at the monastery for that week and only 6 of us were women. I was also obviously the youngest person at this retreat.

The first evening at the monastery had a scheduled 6:30 p.m. talk by the Guestmaster monk who welcomed us and talked a bit about some of the logistics of staying there before he proceeded with his lecture on finding a Living God within you. He told us an interesting story that I want to capture here as it is a great parable for healing.

The story went: "There was a man named Joe who would go to the same pub every day to get a drink. He was not necessarily an alcoholic; he just liked the community feel of the pub. He would always order the same drink and talk to the people at the pub. Everyone knew Joe and Joe knew everyone. One evening Joe sat at the bar and bartender asked if he wanted his usual drink. Joe said yes and the bartender poured him a shot. Then, as Joe looked around the room, he asked the bartender: "Is that who I think it is at the end of the bar? Is that our Lord?" Bartender responded: "Oh yes, it is. Jesus stops by here occasionally". Joe asked the bartender to pour Jesus a drink on him. Then Jesus comes over to Joe and says: "You've been so kind to offer me a drink. Let me heal you as I see that you cannot walk." To that Joe responds: "Jesus, thank you but I don't want you to heal me because I like my disability check that I receive every month." I know, I did not expect this story to come out of the monk's mouth either. However, this is a great story to illustrate how so many people refuse help to heal themselves because it is easier to stay in the same role of a victim that they've played for so long. If Joe were to be healed, then he had to go out and get a job and he no longer could ask everyone for assistance.

Emotional healing is different. One of the toughest things you can do is to seek emotional healing from past experiences. Once you heal emotionally, you can no longer justify your bad behavior that was created by what happened to you. You must break the old patterns and cycles and be reborn from ashes like a phoenix. If it were easy, then everyone would do it. My deepest desire is that sharing my experiences through this book might help someone break free of the invisible chains that are placed around the person by their abusers and their life circumstances. We cannot choose to which family we were born and raised but we can choose the kind of adult we become.

An organization that made a big impact on my life and journey toward forgiving my father is Saprea (www.saprea.org). Their mission is to liberate this world from child sexual abuse. It is a topic that makes most people feel uncomfortable. It's a topic that most people want to avoid and yet one in four children get sexually abused worldwide. Imagine being in crowd and as you look around, realizing that 25% of the people surrounding you were sexually abused as a child. I went to the Saprea gala in 2021. At that gala, for the first time, I publicly announced that I was a thriving survivor of childhood sexual abuse. There was something so liberating about coming out of the shadows of this trauma. It takes on average 30 plus years for a survivor to be able to voice that this horrific thing happened to them. Some people take this "secret" to their graves and never have an opportunity to liberate themselves of the shame that has been forced upon them.

The following year I was invited to serve as part of the gala committee and that was a tremendous honor for me. I remember walking into the first committee meeting thinking that I was an imposter who did not deserve to be given such a responsibility. I am thankful that this fear was not a reality, and I was able to make contributions of my own. I also applied to participate in the four-day retreat for survivors that Saprea organizes weekly at their Utah and Georgia locations. I was blessed to be selected to participate in the retreat in February of 2023 just a few days before the 2023 Saprea International Gala.

I looked at this retreat as my graduation from trauma healing. I have spent so many years in various types of therapy, plus the sabbatical journey I took, and I finally felt like I have left the past in the past. I was curious to see how I would be when surrounded by other survivors and if hearing their stories would have a triggering effect on me. At this point in time, I knew with 100% confidence that I could discuss my own experience without any trace of emotion, but I was not sure that my compassionate heart could bear hearing other women's stories. I did not think I would get much out of this retreat myself, but I was hopeful that I could be an example of hope for women attending the retreat with me. I can admit now that this retreat blew my expectations out of the water.

The minute we joined Saprea employees, we were immediately told to not worry about anything. We were not even allowed to handle our own luggage so that we could begin feeling the sense of care as soon as we walked into the beautiful cabin that was going to be our home for the next 4 days. I have never in my life felt as genuinely taken care of and pampered as I felt here. We had two chefs preparing our meals every day at the level of any 5-star restaurant. We had as many Saprea employees taking care of us as the number of us. Through various sessions and hearing fellow survivors speaks, I felt "normal" for the first time in my life.

Anything I would share; was met with head nods or verbal confirmations that I was not the only one who felt this way or acted that way. I learned that there are common responses that we all shared from time to time. I also realized that my hope to be 100% healed will never come true, that I am on a healing journey and that the perfection that I was seeking does not exist. It is such a liberating feeling to not focus so much on the end goal but instead look at the progress that I have made so far. And in case you were wondering, I did have a triggering moment during the retreat, and it caused me to have a realization.

When I have gone through any crisis in the past, I have ALWAYS gone through it on my own. My response is to close myself off from the rest of the world and people closest to me and process my feelings on my own. Once the peak of the crisis passed, that's when I would reach out to friends for help. I never wanted to be a weak nuisance to people in my life. I shouldered all the pain on my own. For the first time in my life, I have forced myself to stay in the room with other people as I was going through a crisis. As I was talking about it surrounded by women who understood me, I was crying in front of strangers for the first time in my life. In that moment, I was stronger by showing what I used to consider to be a weakness.

That day I made myself a promise that when future crisis comes into my life, I will reach out to a trusted friend instead of keeping it all to myself. Showing my vulnerability is not natural to me but it is something that I need to do as part of my healing journey.

As we were saying goodbye to each other on the last day of the retreat, it was a bittersweet feeling for all of us. We have become a Thrive Tribe. Women who bonded over shared traumatic experiences and became stronger through it. The feeling was that we knew each other for a long time even though it was just a few days. Some people say that time is not linear, and I understood what they mean for the first time in my life. I am so thankful to Saprea for this life changing experience and if you are someone who have experienced sexual abuse as a child reading this book, I hope that you would take this next step in your healing journey and apply to participate in this incredible retreat.

Through my sabbatical journey, I was moved to write this book. One of the biggest questions I had for this week at the monastery was about my book. Was the purpose to shed my past through these written pages and find healing for myself? Was I supposed to share these pages with other people? How should I bring this book to light- through a publisher or by self-publishing it? As it often goes, the answer I received was not exactly the answer I was expecting. Through prayer, I heard that I needed to share my story about this book with everyone I encounter. God will send me a person who will help publish my book. I thought, time will tell when and how this book will come to light but that's the exciting part about trusting God. You know it will happen when it is supposed to happen. Well, 4 months later I talked about my book with an acquaintance over coffee prior to us going to a networking event and she told me that she will introduce me to her friend who specializes in helping authors self-publish books. I met her that evening and now she is the one who is taking me through the entire self-publishing process. How kind was God to tell me to not exert any extra energy because the right person will just show up when the time is right?

Upon my return from the monastery, I immediately decided to officially join my church. Every new member had to attend the New Member Class. There I met a woman who became one of my closest friends and allies in Atlanta. Once Sandy and I met, our friendship blossomed in a beautiful way. We both admitted that we had been praying to find each other and God could not have crafted a match better than what we found in each other. We both shared our stories of singlehood and our decisions to prioritize serving God and the community prior to meeting each other. This connection was what led to us become business partners as well.

One evening we were sitting around my dinner table over noodles when we started talking about how it is tough for us to expand our Christian circle beyond people we meet at church. The median age at the church we attend is currently sixty-one, thus we were craving to meet other young professionals. A Google search for Christian meetups in Atlanta led to zero results as nothing official existed at that time. This is how our organization Christian Professionals of Atlanta (www.cpofatl.com) was born. Within a week, we created an organization with the intent of bringing a community of like-minded individuals who want to grow their Christian circle while focusing on philanthropy.

We quickly realized as we began talking to other people, we would meet at various networking events that we are fulfilling a need that is not currently served in Atlanta and across the nation. It is too early to tell what our growth trajectory will be, but we aspire to build an organization that will be called Christian Professionals of America with chapters in most large metropolitan areas. Now I live with a newly invigorated purpose that excites me and I know that my work will make meaningful positive impact on this world.

Now looking back at my sabbatical journey, I am so thankful that everything worked out the way that it did. I have learned so many valuable lessons in such a short period of time and have created through it something that is so much bigger than me. Something that will hopefully live beyond my life on this Earth and continue to bring positive impact into lives of many people. If you are going through a difficult time in your life that you don't understand, I recommend you look at the situation and try to understand what that lesson is supposed to teach you. Trust that everything in life happens for a reason and look for the lesson in it and look for the good that it will ultimately bring into your life. My courage has allowed me to now live the life I never knew would be possible for me. If I won the lottery tomorrow and did not have to work one day in my life, I would still continue doing what I am doing now. This is how you know that you are fulfilling your purpose and you found your true happiness. There is nothing else out there that I am searching for to validate me or make me happy. Everything that I need is within me. Each person is capable of finding this courage to change. I encourage you to take that first step and see what happens.

Finding Courage to Change

Acknowledgements

I want to thank God for giving me the guidance and inspiration to write this book. My purpose in life is to fulfill the mission that You have bestowed upon me. My hope is that this book will provide hope and inspiration. Even in the darkest moment, there is always hope. I am thankful to my host families for showing me an example of what a loving family is. I am thankful to my friends who fill my life with love and joy. I am thankful to myself for having the courage to go through this journey once again as I was writing the book.

Finding Courage to Change

Appendix: List of Recommended Books

The Success Principles by Jack Canfield

The 5 Second Rule by Mel Robbins

Attached by Amir Levine and Rachel Heller

The Circle Maker by Mark Batterson

Never Split the Difference by Chris Voss

The 4-hour Workweek by Timothy Ferriss

Act like a Lady, Think like a Man by Steve Harvey

Game Changers by Dave Asprey

Lioness Arising by Lisa Bevere

Dare to Lead by Brené Brown

The Tipping Point by Malcolm Gladwell

The Four Agreements by don Miguel Ruiz

It Starts with Food by Melissa Hartwig and Dallas Hartwig

Start with Why by Simon Sinek

12 Rules for Life by Jordan B Peterson

Finding Courage to Change

Becoming Supernatural by Dr. Joe Dispenza

Grit by Angela Duckworth

Becoming a Dangerous Woman by Pat Mitchell

Love Does by Bob Goff

Never Too Far by Louie Giglio

The Laws of Human Nature by Robert Greene

Blink by Malcolm Gladwell

Influence by Robert B. Cialdini

The Code of the Extraordinary Mind by Vishen Lakhiani

The Happiness Advantage by Shawn Achor

Atlas of the Heart by Brené Brown

Greenlights by Matthew McConaughey

Think Like a Monk by Jay Shetty

The Culture Code by Daniel Coyle

Art of Seduction by Robert Greene

The Compound Effect by Darren Hardy

Can't Hurt Me by David Goggins

Misbehaving by Richard H Thaler

What If? By Randall Munroe

Finding Courage to Change

Finding Courage to Change

Finding Courage to Change

Made in the USA
Columbia, SC
20 June 2024

37095927R00078